Jacke

Sl

G000271494

4

Maureen Goldsworthy

Mills & Boon Ltd
London   Sydney   Toronto

I am most grateful to Rosamund Keer and my daughter Alice Helps who modelled the jackets. I should also like to thank Jill Hilyer who made the jacket on page 10, and Robert Saunders of Wright Photography who took the photographs at Warwick Castle, by kind permission of Warwick Castle Ltd.

For A.F.F.

First published in 1980

© Maureen Goldsworthy 1980

ISBN 0 263 06428 X

Designed by Richard Brown Associates

Printed in Great Britain by
Fletcher & Son Ltd, Norwich

and bound by
Richard Clay (The Chaucer Press) Ltd,
Bungay, Suffolk

for the publishers Mills & Boon Ltd,
15–16 Brooks Mews,
London W1Y 1LF

CONTENTS

INTRODUCTION

Most people who make their own clothes are quite happy to run up a blouse or a dress, but may hesitate to take on a jacket, which threatens to combine every dressmaking complexity from interfacing and lining to the setting on of a collar and the making of buttonholes. But if you have done a certain amount of dressmaking, and are used to working accurately, then there is no reason at all why you should not be equally successful with a jacket.

The jacket shown on page 10 was actually the first to be made by someone good at dressmaking who had not previously attempted a jacket.

The real problem is with the fit, and therefore with the pattern. If you use a commercial pattern, the disadvantage is that it will be in a stock size while you may not. So you are faced with having to alter the pattern; for a fitted jacket, the alterations may be extensive. However, by drafting your personal block patterns, based on no fewer than ten of your own measurements, an exact fit at every point can be assured. All your future jacket patterns, of whatever style, are derived from the permanent record of the blocks.

The first section of this book covers the drafting of the basic blocks. The next part shows how to translate them into a working pattern for the design you have chosen, which can be in any style from the classically fitted to the most casual. The last section gives full instructions for making up.

Making your own patterns does take a little time. You will probably need two or three hours to draft the blocks, then another two or three to make the final pattern with all the styling details. But if you can follow an ordinary dressmaking pattern, you should have no trouble with these instructions. The system of drafting used here will give you an accurate fit: that is the most important point.

But it is also a much simpler system than most, because the blocks have been planned just for the shape of a single type of garment – the jacket.

So take the instructions as they come. There are no hidden horrors lying in wait.

4

Paper

Squared dressmaker's paper is expensive and may be difficult to find. It is much better to use a roll of ceiling lining paper. This is strong, easily obtainable and quite wide enough. Besides, you will need plenty of it and it is cheap.

Thin card

This is obtainable from art stationers. Four sheets will be needed for the final pattern blocks.

Set square

This is handy but not essential. Without one, lines at exact right angles to the edge of the paper can be made by creasing. When you fold across the width of the paper, keep the side edges exactly level with each other; the creases will then be at right angles to the side edges (*Figure 1*).

Tracing wheel

A wheel with sharp *metal* points, used to transfer pattern outlines from an upper to a lower sheet of paper. Obtainable in haberdashery (US notions) departments (*Figure 2*). A plastic wheel will not do.

Carbon paper

This is for transferring double-thickness markings.

Pencils

Hard pencils (H or 2H). Coloured fibre-tip pens are also useful.

Long ruler or straight edge

Tape measure

This should be marked in centimetres. If you have not yet tried working in centimetres, this is the time to do so. The metric system is actually much easier to use than the imperial system, and you should not attempt to convert one to the other; this is why alternative inch measurements are not given. Just take the centimetres as they come – one soon gets over the shock of one's hip measurement hovering around the hundred mark.

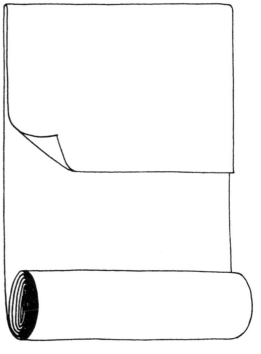

Figure 1

Figure 2

5

PERSONAL MEASUREMENT CHART

Ten body measurements are needed for constructing the block patterns. You must have the help of a friend to measure you; it is impossible to do this accurately for yourself.

Measurements should be taken closely but not tightly. The extra ease needed for movement in the jacket should not be allowed for, as it is built into the blocks (*Figure 3*).

1 Bust, taken over the fullest part. At the back keep the tape measure high across the shoulder blades_____cm
Quarter bust measurement_____cm
One-twelfth bust measurement_____cm

2 Waist_____cm

3 Hip, taken over the widest part of the hip, usually 20–22 cm below the waist____cm
Quarter hip measurement_____cm

4 Hip depth, the measurement from waist down to the widest part of the hips, taken down the side_____cm

5 Back width, taken 10 cm below the prominent bone at the nape of the neck, from one armhole seam to the other. If in doubt, be generous here_____cm
Half back width_____cm

6 Back waist length, taken from the prominent bone at the nape down to the waistline. (Tie a piece of string round the waist to show its true level.)_____cm
Half back waist length_____cm
Quarter back waist length_____cm

7 Bust point width, the measurement between the points of the bust_____cm
Half bust point width_____cm

8 Shoulder to bust point length, taken from the centre of the shoulder seam down to the point of the bust_____cm

9 Arm length, taken from the shoulder bone to the wrist bone, round the elbow, with the arm slightly bent. Be generous here_____cm

10 Arm girth, taken round the fullest part of the upper arm_____cm

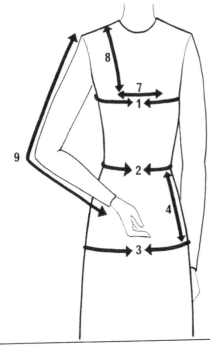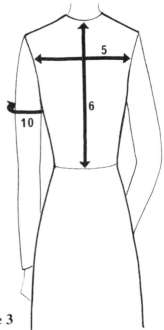

Figure 3

DRAFTING THE BLOCKS

Block patterns are not fashion shapes and contain no styling. Nor do they include seam and hem allowances; so they cannot be used directly as dressmaking patterns. They are simply the essential record of your bone structure, from which the final pattern is built. Even changes in your weight will not substantially affect the fit. A couple of centimetres more, or less, on hip or bust or waist, just means that you need to add or subtract a quarter of that amount on the side seam edges of the final pattern – which you can do without cutting a new block. The blocks provide, however, a permanent fit for the important measurements across the back, and down the back from neck to waist, on which the proportions of the pattern depend.

DRAWING CURVES
Pattern drafting consists mainly of measuring and ruling straight lines, but sometimes you will need to draw curved lines joining three or more points. Here is the simplest way to draw a smooth curve.

Always draw from the inside of the curve, so that the movement of your hand goes naturally with the line rather than against it. If you draw as shown in *Figure 4*, you will have less control over your pencil, and the line may wobble. But turn the paper round, draw as shown in *Figure 5*, and the movement of your hand will then assist the curve.

For a full curve, rest the heel of your hand on the paper and use it as a pivot. For a very shallow curve, use your elbow as a pivot. Draw quickly: the curve will be smoother than if you tense your fingers and go slowly.

FOLDING IN DARTS
It is easy to draw in the two sides of a dart; less easy to shape the seamline from which the dart springs. The following method is foolproof, and should be used for darts in any part of a garment.

1 Draw in the provisional seamline as a straight line, A–B (*Figure 6*). Mark in the two sides of the dart, C–D and E–D.

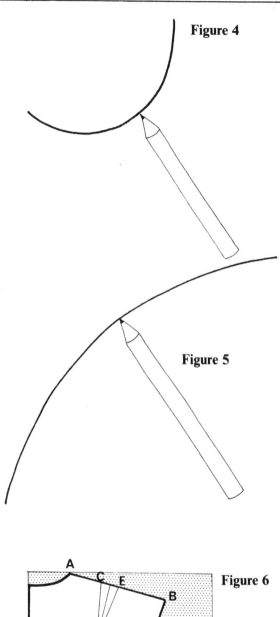

Figure 4

Figure 5

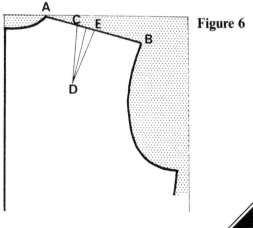

Figure 6

2 Lay the paper across the corner of a table, with the lower part of the pattern hanging over the edge. With the point of the dart – D – on the corner of the table, crease the pattern from C to D and bring the crease over to the line E–D, matching the sides of the dart accurately (*Figure 7*).

3 This folding will bend the seamline; so, still with the dart folded, rule a new straight line between A and B. Cut along this line and unfold the dart. *Figure 8* shows the shape of the final seamline.

DRAFTING THE BACK BLOCK
Cut a rectangle of lining paper:

Length: back waist length plus hip depth, plus 3 cm.
Width: a quarter of hip measurement, plus 1 cm.
Mark A at the top left-hand corner, as in *Figure 9*.
Measuring down the left-hand edge:

A–B is 2 cm;
B–C is 2 cm;
B–D is a quarter of back waist length;
B–E is half back waist length plus 2·5 cm;
B–F is back waist length plus 1 cm.

Crease the paper right across from C, D, E and F, making sure that the creases are parallel to the top edge.
Mark G at the bottom left-hand corner.
Measuring along the creases:

A–H is one-twelfth of bust measurement;
C–J is half back width, plus 2 cm;
D–K is half back width, plus 1 cm;
Mark L at the mid-point of D–K;
E–M is the same as D–K;
E–N is one quarter bust measurement, plus 1 cm;
F–P is one quarter bust measurement, minus 1 cm;
G–Q is the same length as D–L;
Mark R at the bottom right-hand corner.

For the neckline
Join B–H in a shallow curve; this line is horizontal for the first 2 cm.

For the shoulderline and darts
Join H–J for the provisional shoulderline.
H–S is 6·5 cm
Join S–L. T is 7·5 cm from S, down this line.
U and V are 0·5 cm to each side of S.
Join U–T–V for the shoulder dart.
Now fold in dart, as shown in *Figures 6, 7* and *8*. Rule a line from H to J across the fold, cut along the line and unfold the dart. This gives the final shoulderline.

Join L–Q for the position of any back waist dart you may wish to make later.

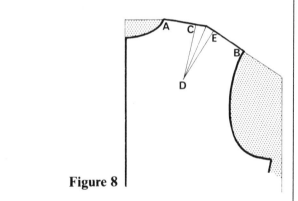

Figure 8

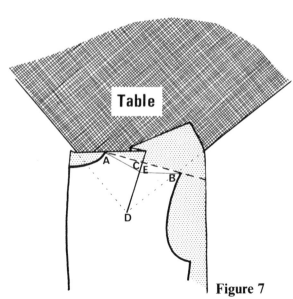

Table

Figure 7

DRAFTING THE BLOCKS

For the armhole

Join K–M.

Draw a diagonal line 2·5 cm long, from M to W.

Join J–K–W–N in a smooth curve. (J–K is slightly hollowed; K–W is almost straight for half its length, then the line curves fully to N.)

For the side seam

Join N–P–R

Draw a shallow curve from P to R, up to 0·5 cm out from the straight line.

Balance marks

Mark a notch at P, and at each side of the shoulder dart. Mark a double notch at K.

Cut out the block

Discard the shaded areas shown on the diagram.

DRAFTING THE FRONT BLOCK

Cut a rectangle of paper the same length but 8 cm wider than the piece you cut for the back block.

Crease right down the paper, 2 cm from the left-hand edge (*Figure 10*). Place the back block on the paper, with its left-hand edge matched to the crease, with the lower edges level, and with H (the neck point of the shoulderline) touching the top edge.

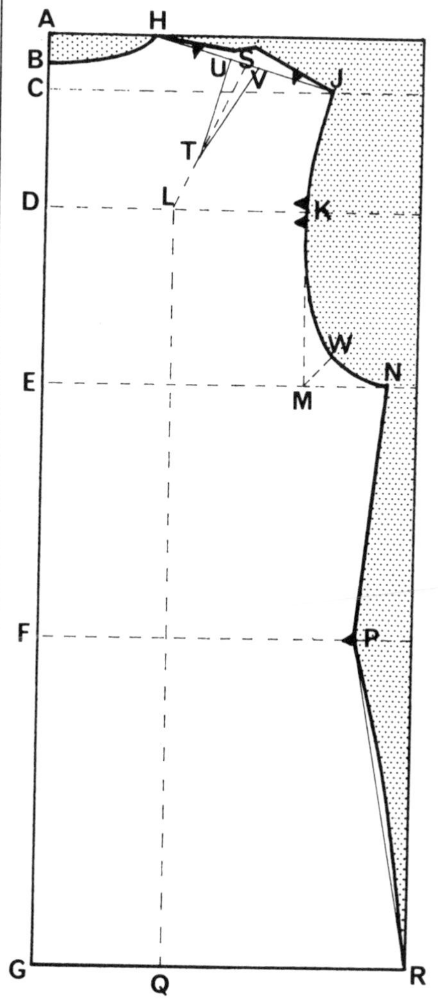

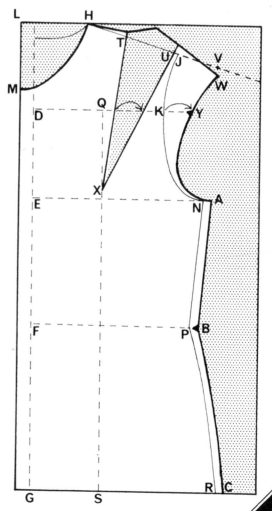

Figure 9

Figure 10

As shown by the thin line, draw all round the block, except for the shoulderline H–J. Here, join H–J with a straight line for the moment.

Draw in the lines D–K, E–N and F–P.

Mark in the points G and R.

Remove the back block.

For the side seam
Draw in the side seam 1 cm to the right of the line N–P–R, and mark in A, B and C as shown.

For the neckline
Mark L at the top left-hand corner of the paper.

L–M down the left-hand edge is 0·5 cm *less* than the front neck width L–H.

Join M–H for the front neckline; this is almost a quarter circle.

For the waist dart
D–Q is half bust point width.

G–S is half bust point width.

Join Q–S to give the position of any front waist dart you may wish to add later.

For the shoulder shaping
Extend the line H–J to the edge of the paper.

Measuring along this line:
H–T is 6 cm;
T–U (the width of the bust dart) is 2 cm *less* than the front neck width L–H;
J–V (along the extended line) is 1 cm *less* than the length of T–U.

Measure 1 cm down from V and mark W.

For the bust dart
Measure the shoulder to bust point length from T down to X, letting X fall on the line running down from Q to S. This gives one side of the dart.

Join U–X for the other side.

Jacket with drawstring waist

Fold in dart as shown in *Figures 6, 7* and *8,* redraw shoulder as a straight line from H to W, cut along this line and unfold the dart.

Check that the back and front shoulders (less their darts) are the same length.

For the armhole
Measure the width of the dart at the level of the line D–K (shown by the arrow).

Extend D–K to the right by the same measurement as the width of the dart, and mark Y.

Joint W–Y–A for the front armhole. (W–Y is almost straight; Y–A is a full curve.)

Balance marks
Mark notches at B and Y.

Cut out the block
Discard the shaded areas shown on the diagram.

DRAFTING THE SLEEVE BLOCK

Cut a rectangle of paper:
Length: arm length plus 1 cm.
Width: arm girth plus 7 cm.

Figure 11 Crease down centre. Mark A at top of crease. Crease sides-to-middle, so that the edges meet on the first crease, from A downwards.

Open out the paper.

On the back and front jacket blocks, measure the armhole curves J–N (*Figure 9*) and W–A (*Figure 10*). This is easiest if you measure with the tape on its edge, so that it can follow the curve (*Figure 12*). Add these two measurements together to obtain the armhole girth.

Divide the armhole girth by three; this length (about 14–15 cm) will be the sleevehead depth.

Measure this length down the left-hand edge of the paper and mark B.

Crease across the paper to C.

Join B–A–C.

Mark D and E where these lines cross the creases.

To shape the sleevehead

Measure to the midpoint of B–D, then measure 0·5 cm inside the line and mark F.

Measure 1 cm outside the line at D and mark G.

Measure to the midpoint of D–A, then measure 2 cm outside the line and mark H.

Measure to the midpoint of A–E, then measure 2·5 cm outside the line and mark J.

Measure 1 cm outside E and mark K.

Measure to the midpoint of E–C, then measure 1·5 cm inside the line and mark L.

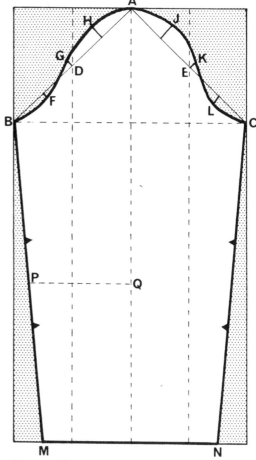

Figure 11

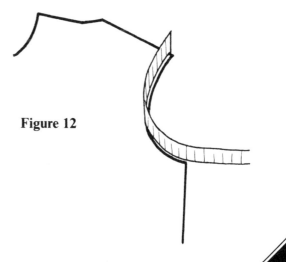

Figure 12

11

DRAFTING THE BLOCKS

Draw in the sleevehead through the points B–F–G–H–A–J–K–L–C. (The curve is shallower at the back of the sleevehead between B and A, more pronounced at the front of the sleevehead between A and C.)

To shape the sleeve
From the bottom corners of the paper, measure 5 cm inwards and mark M and N.

Join B–M for the back edge of the sleeve and C–N for the front edge.

For the elbow line
Mark P at the midpoint of B–M. Crease across from P to Q on the centre crease. This is the position for any elbow dart you may wish to make later on.

Balance marks
Mark notches above and below P; fold the sleeve in half down the centre-line and mark corresponding notches on the other edge.

Cut out the block
Discard the shaded areas.

CHECKING THE CURVES
The back and front
1 Place the back and front blocks together along the shoulder seam, matching at their neck ends. There should be an unbroken curve round the neckline. Re-cut (only a millimetre or two) if needed to smooth out the curve (*Figure 13*). Mark a notch on the front shoulder to match the back notch.

2 Now match the shoulder lines at their armhole ends, check and if necessary re-cut to smooth out the curve there. Mark a notch on the front shoulder to match the second notch on the back (*Figure 14*).

3 Match the sides of the blocks, from the armhole downwards; check for a smooth curve under the armhole (*Figure 15*).

The sleeve
1 Fold the sleeve block edges-to-middle, matching B to C and M to N. Check the smoothness of the underarm curve.

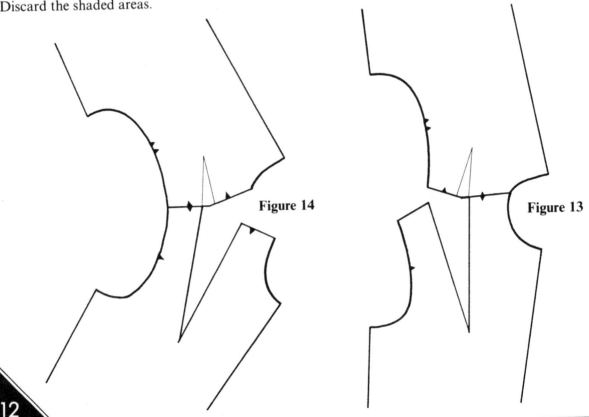

Figure 14

Figure 13

DRAFTING THE BLOCKS

2 With the sleeve still folded in half, rule a line from the bottom of the back-arm fold, through M, to the front-arm fold (*Figure 16*). Cut along this line and unfold the block. The wristline will now be correctly shaped (*Figure 17*).

3 Now place the sleeve and back blocks *right sides together,* matching the underarm points (*Figure 18*). Following the curves, swing the sleevehead round the lower part of the bodice armhole until K is reached. Mark a pair of corresponding notches on the sleevehead. (The double notch will distinguish the back edge of the sleeve, and make it impossible to sew the wrong sleeve into the wrong armhole – otherwise an easy trap for the unwary.)

4 Repeat with the front block and the front edge of the sleevehead, placed as in *Figure 19*, and mark a notch level with Y.

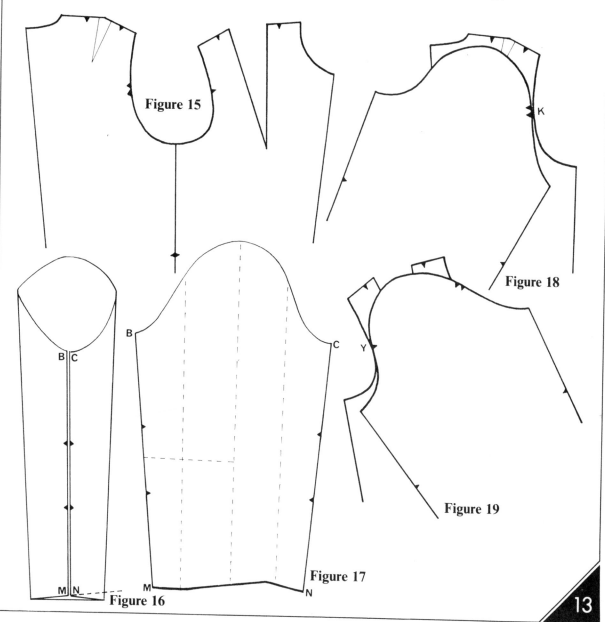

Figure 15

Figure 18

Figure 16

Figure 17

Figure 19

FITTING THE BLOCKS

Since the fit of a jacket is of such importance, it would be well worth your while to make up the blocks – just as they are, without any styling – from a piece of an old sheet. It will take very little time, but may save you from having to make more difficult and time-consuming adjustments on the fabric itself. Any alterations made now are transferred to the blocks, so will not need to be done over again when you make your next jacket.

1 Place the blocks on a double thickness of the sheeting, or any other firmly-woven fabric such as calico. The back block should be placed to a straight-grain fold (*Figure 20*). Draw round the blocks, then add *2·5 cm* seam allowances along the shoulders, and normal 1·5 cm allowances along the armhole and side seams, and down the centre-front (so that the front opening can be pinned together). Do not add any seam allowance round the neck or at the hemline. Mark in the lines for the shoulder darts and for the waist darts (L–Q on the back block and X–S on the front as shown in *Figures 9* and *10*).

2 Cut out, but do not cut down the front dart shaping.

3 Similarly, mark out the right sleeve (i.e. with the block face-upwards). Add 1·5 cm seam allowances round the sleevehead and down the sides of the sleeve.

4 With the longest machine-stitch, machine-baste the back and front shoulder darts; the front dart is tapered to finish 3 cm above its marked point (for a reason that will become apparent shortly).

5 Machine-baste the shoulder and side seams. The extra turnings along the shoulders may be needed for adjustments during fitting.

6 Machine-baste the sleeve underarm seam.

7 Try on the bodice only – not the sleeve – over a dress or jersey. If you intend to have shoulder pads, pin them now inside whichever you are wearing. Pin together the front opening.

Fitting the neckline

Check that the neckline lies smoothly, without pulling round the neck. If it is too tight, with wrinkles running up to the neck edge as in *Figure 21,* mark a new neckline a few millimetres lower round the back and sides of the neck and cut along the marking.

If the back neck only is too tight, unpick the shoulder seams and re-pin as in *Figure 22*, moving more fabric into the centre-back. This will leave narrower seam allowances at the back of the armhole.

Pencil in the new neck and armhole seamlines.

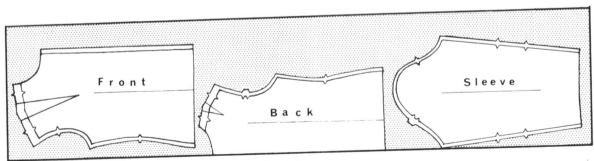

Figure 20

The pitch

Does the jacket hang straight? The pitch may
be faulty because of a rounded back, in which
case the back of the jacket will hang outwards
(*Figure 23*). This is corrected by adding length
at the level of the shoulder-blades. Cut right
across the back between the armhole notches.
Pin a strip of fabric under the slash, but do
not add any length at the armhole. You are
unlikely to need an addition of more than 1 cm.
2 cm would be exceptional, for a stooped
figure. *Figure 24* shows how the added length
will mean the widening of the back shoulder
dart.

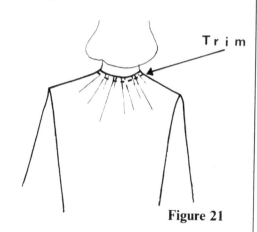

Trim

Figure 21

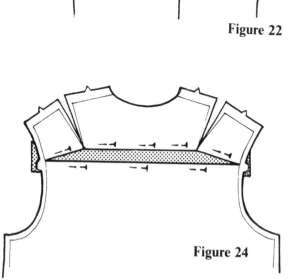

Figure 22

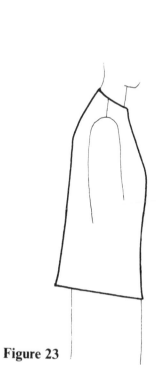

Figure 23

Figure 24

If the jacket pokes out in front, below a prominent bust, then extra length needs to be added to the front. This can be done by slashing, as for the back; but it is simpler to drop the whole front from the neckline by re-pinning the shoulder seam to take in a narrower seam allowance towards the neck end of the seam (*Figure 25*).

Fitting the shoulders
Check now the slope of the shoulder line. If your shoulders are square, you may find creases pulling downwards from the point of the shoulder (*Figure 26*). To correct this fault, let out the shoulder seam a little towards the armhole end, and pin it with narrower seam turnings. Do not alter the neck end of the seam.

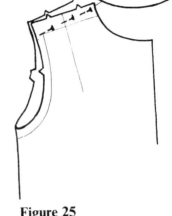

Figure 25

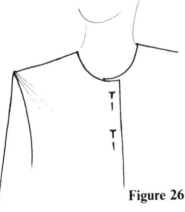

Figure 26

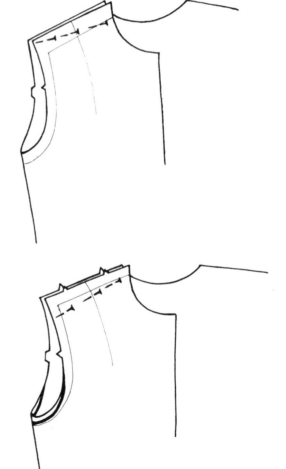

Figure 27

If your shoulders are sloping, you may see a fold drooping from the neck to below the shoulder (*Figure 27*). The remedy is to lift the seam at the shoulder and pin it to take in wider turnings towards the armhole end. This will mean trimming off an equal amount from the lower edge of the armhole.

Check that your shoulders are *level*; many people have one shoulder higher than the other. It is better to level up the lower one with a little extra padding, rather than to make any alteration to one shoulder seam.

Now look at the *length* of the shoulder seam. The sleevehead seam should cross it 1 cm beyond the point of the shoulder – where you can feel the bone. Mark this point if necessary, so that you can set in the sleeve at that level.

Fitting the waist
Lastly, consider how much fitting is needed to the waist. The blocks give only a slightly shaped waistline – 8 cm less than the bust measurement of the jacket. If you need more fitting than this, pin darts as shown in *Figure 28* down the side-front (*Figure 10*, X–S) and side-back (*Figure 9*, L–Q). From the waistline, they should taper to nothing below the bust and above the hemline; usually, waist darts are slightly shorter above than below the waist. Do not over-fit: the jacket should move easily on the figure.

Fitting the sleeve
Tack the sleeve into the right armhole, matching the notches and placing the centre of the sleevehead to the shoulder seam. Try on.

The sleeve should hang without pulling at the point of the shoulder. If creases are apparent, as in *Figure 29*, let out a little of the sleevehead seam allowance to give a fraction more length. If, on the other hand, loose folds form below the point of the shoulder (*Figure 30*), this indicates that the sleevehead is too deep. Re-pin with a wider seam allowance.

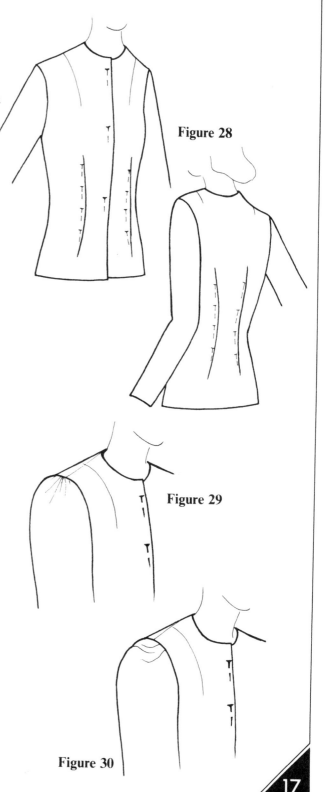

Figure 28

Figure 29

Figure 30

Check the length; with the elbow bent, a full-length sleeve should come to the wristbone.

Creases or folds at the sides of the sleeve are a sign that it has been tacked into the armhole a little askew: they do not call for any alteration to the pattern.

Corrections to the blocks

Any corrections you have made on the fabric model should now be made on the blocks themselves. Also cut out the bust dart shaping from the front block (T–X–U, *Figure 10*). Once this is done, jacket patterns of any style can in future be cut from the blocks without preliminary fitting.

TRANSFERRING THE BLOCKS TO CARD

Now that the blocks are in their final form, you should transfer their outlines on to sheets of thin card, as a permanent record.

The back

Place the back block over a sheet of card and draw accurately round its outline (*Figure 31*). With the tracing wheel, mark in with perforations:
the dart;
the line L–Q, which serves as a straight-grain line;
any dart shaping constructed on this line;
the line F–P, the waist level.

Cut out the block, cut the notches inwards, and label the block with its name.

The front

Place the front block over a sheet of card and draw round its edges. With the tracing wheel, mark in *heavily* (so that the marks will show on the reverse of the card):
the line X–S, which serves as a straight-grain line;
any dart shaping constructed on this line;
the line F–B, the waist level.

Cut out the card block, turn it over and label it (*Figure 32*). From now on, that side of the block is used as the right side – in both senses. It now relates to the right-hand side of the body, and corresponds to the back block – which also relates to the right-hand side of the body.

The sleeve

Draw round the outline over card (*Figure 33*). Mark in:
the centre line as a straight-grain line;
the elbow-dart line P–Q and the back-arm line below it;
the line B–C.

As the sleeve is already drafted for the right arm, your blocks form a complete record for that side of the body.

The blocks are now ready to be used for developing whatever style of jacket you may want. They themselves are not working patterns, but templets: they are never cut or altered in any way. The final pattern, with all the design details as well as the seam and hem allowances, will be traced from them.

The blocks will last indefinitely. Drafting them is a once-for-all operation. To store them, punch a hole near the top of each block, thread a piece of tape through the holes and hang them from a coathanger. As your collection of blocks for different types of garment grows, the coathangers can be hung flat at the back of a wardrobe where they will take up no space.

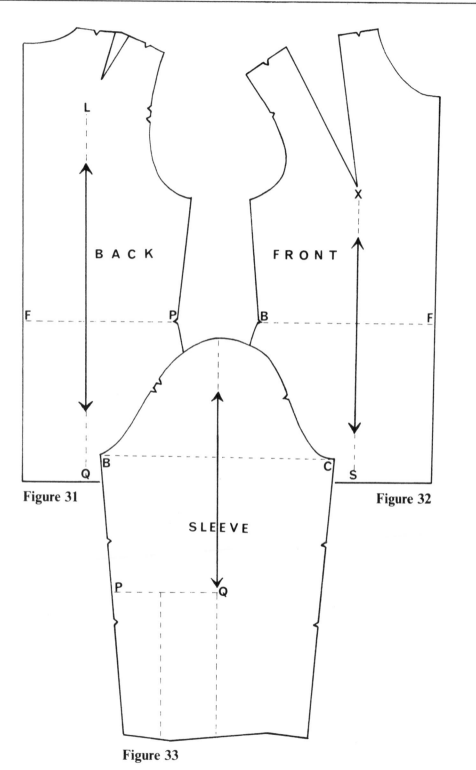

L

B A C K

F   P   B   F

B   C

Q

Figure 31

F R O N T

X

S

Figure 32

S L E E V E

P   Q

Figure 33

DESIGNING THE PATTERN

The next step is to consider what style of jacket you want to develop from the blocks.

Is it to be loose and casual – possibly even unlined – or a fitted jacket to top a matching skirt, such as the one shown here? Is it even to be yoked and flared and quite unstructured, as in the photograph on page 23? The possibilities are endless.

This section gives instructions for cutting a wide variety of styles. Rather than read the whole section, it is suggested that you just browse through the diagrams for ideas. In *Figure 34*, there is a group of body outlines; on thin paper placed over these, you could trace and sketch out the effect of different collar, sleeve and pocket styles, until you have evolved a complete design. Then, simply pick out the instructions for the particular details you need, and disregard the rest.

Take plenty of time deciding: it is quite easy at this stage to work out a pattern for any design – much more difficult, and possibly wasteful in material, to change your ideas later on.

THE DRAFT PATTERN

You do not use the blocks directly as patterns. You simply draw round their outlines on fresh paper, and on those add any styling you want. This often means cutting the draft pattern (not the block) into pieces, to add a yoke seam, or fullness to the back, front or sleeve; if so, the final outline is drawn round the cut pieces on yet another sheet of paper. Lastly, seam and hem allowances are added and the final pattern cut out. Examples of the whole process are the photographs on pages 45 and 46, which show the development of the pattern for the flared jacket on page 23.

The sequence of designing the different parts of the jacket should be:

1 The body shaping – darts, panel seams, yoke seams.

Suit jacket in worsted

2 The collar and facings.

3 The length and hem finish.

4 The sleeves.

5 The pockets.

The instructions that follow are therefore given in this order.

20

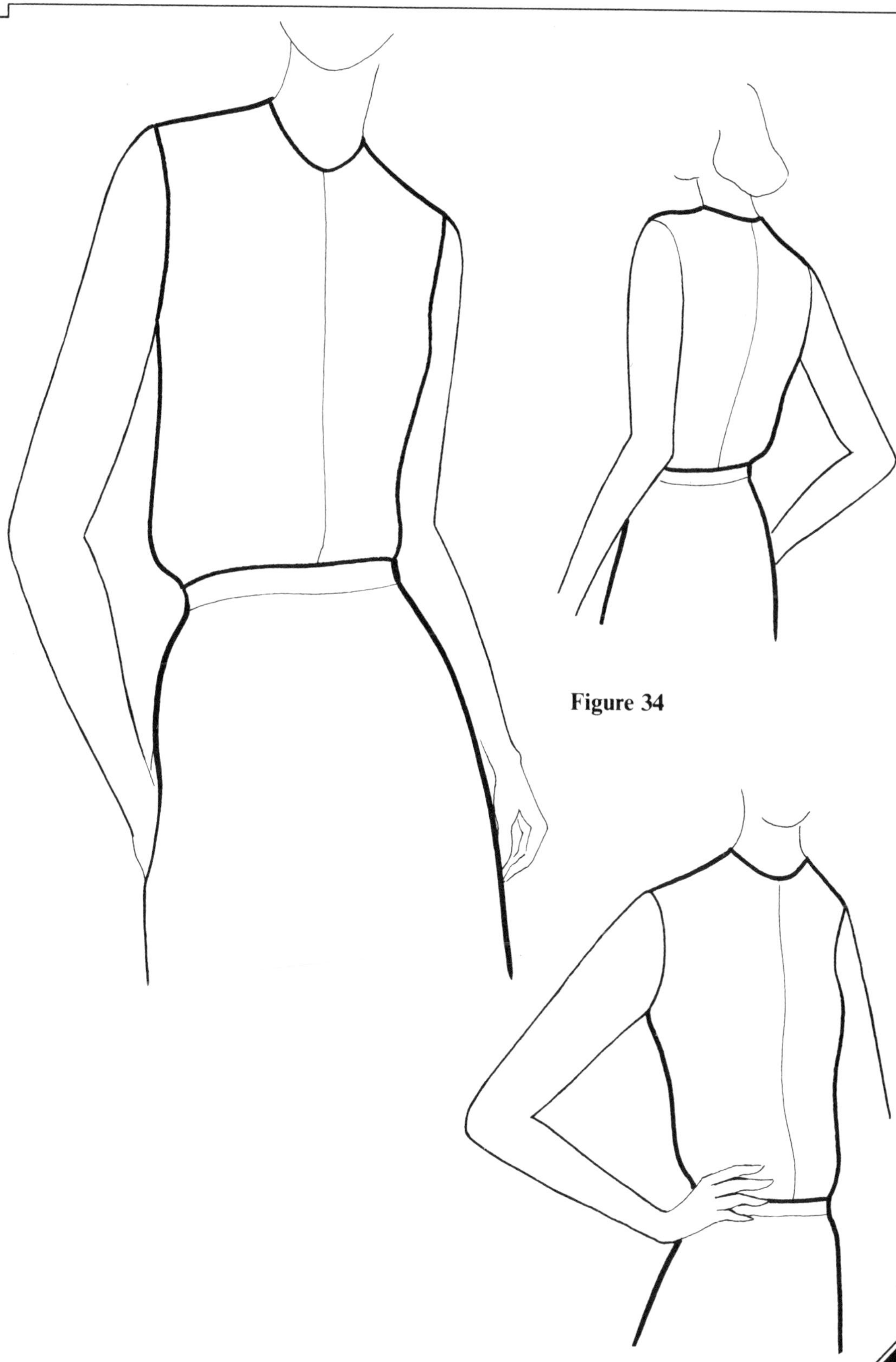

Figure 34

DESIGNING THE PATTERN

THE BODY SHAPING

Darts

In the block, the bust dart (which shapes the front) is drawn from the shoulder seam. This is the most convenient position for it in most jackets. Just draw round the block without making any alterations.

But the dart can if you wish be moved to the side seam. It would then leave an unbroken line across the front of the shoulder, and would be a better pattern for use with checks or stripes.

1 Trace the front block outline on to paper and cut it out.

2 Rule a line from the side seam slightly upwards to the point of the dart. Cut along this line (*Figure 35*).

3 Move the armhole part of the draft pattern round to close the shoulder dart; this will open up a side dart.

4 Draw the new outline on fresh paper.

The dart is drawn to the point of the bust in order that it can be pivoted round into another seam if necessary. It is *not* stitched to that length, but shortened 3 cm to leave more fabric at the point and give a more rounded shape. For the final fitting-line redraw the dart as shown in *Figure 36*.

Development of the flared sleeve pattern for the jacket shown on page 23

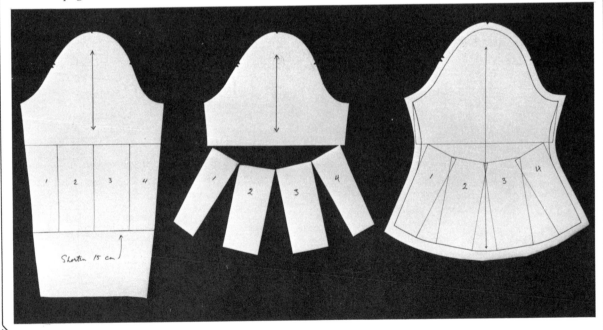

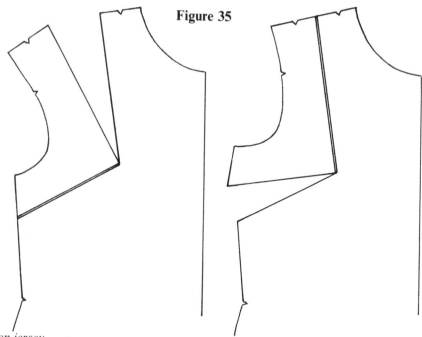

Figure 35

Yoked and flared jacket in cotton jersey

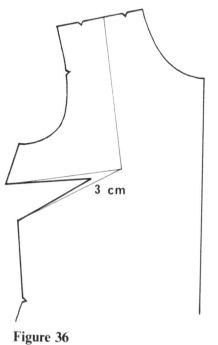

3 cm

Figure 36

DESIGNING THE PATTERN

Panel seams

If you prefer, the body shaping can be achieved by seaming instead of by darts. This can give a smoother line, especially on thick fabrics, and is better if you are planning a close fit. *Figure 37* shows how to separate the back and front into panels, down the dart fitting lines. Mark notches as shown on both sides of the seams.

Front yokes

A yoke can be used simply to introduce a contrasting fabric, without any extra fullness being added below it. You could, for instance, choose a plain fabric for the jacket, with a check for the yoke, collar and revers – and perhaps for a skirt as well.

1 Trace round the block and cut out. Transfer the shoulder dart to the side seam, as above.

2 Mark the line of the yoke seam, which may be straight or curved, and cut along that line (*Figure 38*).

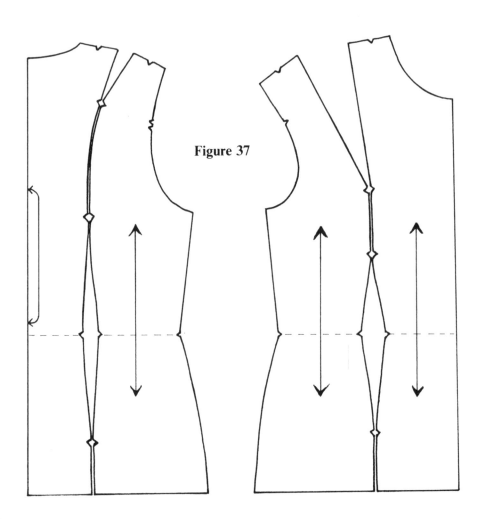

Figure 37

DESIGNING THE PATTERN

The fullness of a flared style can be introduced below a yoke, as in the jacket photographed on page 23. The development of this pattern from the block onwards is shown in the photographs on pages 45 and 46, and is carried out as follows:

1 Trace round the front block as far down as necessary for the length of the jacket, which might be little below the waist. The side seam should be cut straight, not curved in.

2 Fold out the bust dart, and draw the yoke seam across it.

3 Cut the lower part of the draft pattern into sections.

4 Place these sections to touch at their upper edges, but to flare out at the hemline; the overlap of sections two and three compensates for the tip of the dart, the rest having been folded out of the yoke.

5 Draw round the new outlines. The addition of the seam and hem allowances is made later, when all the pattern pieces are ready.

For gathered styles (possible only in soft fabrics, either woven or knitted), cut and spread apart the sections as shown in *Figure 39*. It will probably be enough to leave 5 cm between them. Draw round the yoke and lower section, and mark notches as shown.

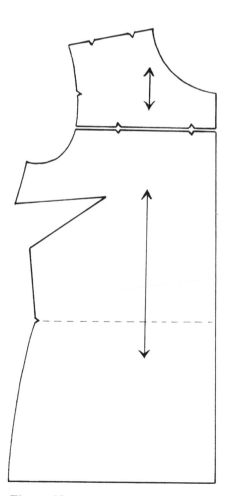

Figure 38

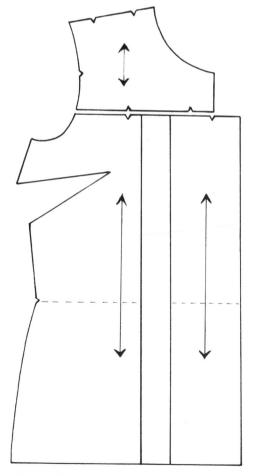

Figure 39

Back yokes

A straight back yoke is often used with a centre-back pleat. It should be cut to replace the back shoulder dart.

1 Mark the yoke line and cut along it (*Figure 40*).

2 Fold in the dart (*Figure 41*). Mark A at the armhole, 1 cm below the yoke line.

3 Trim off a wedge 7·5 cm long, from A towards the centre-back. Transfer this wedge to the yoke (*Figure 42*). The sloping line now left at the armhole will exactly replace the dart shaping, while retaining a straight lower edge to the yoke.

4 For a centre-back pleat, add double its intended width to the centre-back of the lower section. This addition would usually be between 5 and 8 cm (*Figure 43*). Mark crease lines and fold arrow as shown. In this illustration the yoke, being deeper, retains its dart.

THE COLLAR AND FACINGS

The character of a jacket depends on the type and proportion of the collar, and this in turn is largely determined by the level to which the jacket is buttoned. So before drafting any collar, the position of the buttonholes and the width of the overlap must be decided.

For a classic fitted or semi-fitted jacket, the top buttonhole could be about 15 cm below the neckline; but its exact level is a question of taste and the prevailing fashion. One buttonhole should fall at the waistline.

If you choose a buttonless, edge-to-edge style, such as the jacket photographed on page 23, there will of course be no overlap – the centre-front of the jacket will coincide with the opening edges. But for a buttoned style, the total overlap should be 4–6 cm wide; the heavier the fabric, the wider the overlap should be. Half of this width is added to the

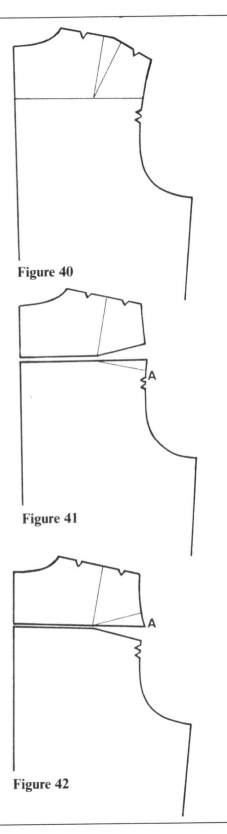

Figure 40

Figure 41

Figure 42

pattern, as the stand for buttons or buttonholes. (Double-breasted styles need an overlap of 10–20 cm, so the button-stand should be 5–10 cm.)

1 On fresh paper, draw round the front pattern as you have developed it so far, allowing about 20 cm spare paper above and to the right of the pattern.

2 Add the width of the button-stand to the centre-front edge (*Figure 44*).

3 Mark the positions of the buttonholes.

Now you are ready to draft any type of collar, revers and facings.

The diagrams may look daunting; but followed step by step they really do work out quite easily.

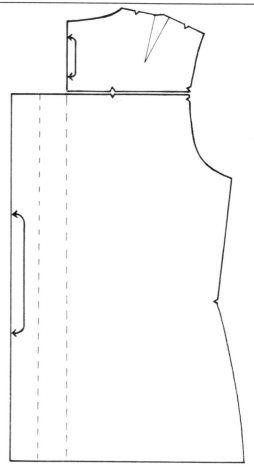

Figure 43

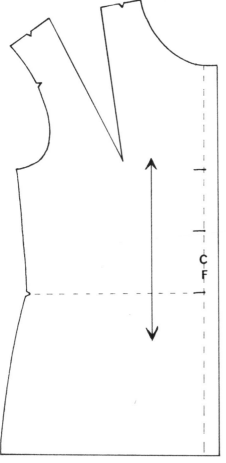

Figure 44

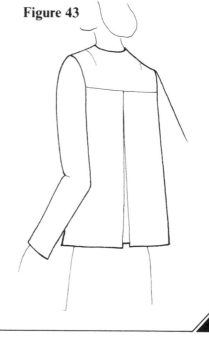

Simple revers front

This simplest of all collars is just an extension of the front neckline and opening edge. It can vary in shape, as shown in *Figure 45*. There is no continuation of the collar across the back of the neck. This type of collar would be a good choice for a first attempt at making a jacket – or if you want to wear it tomorrow.

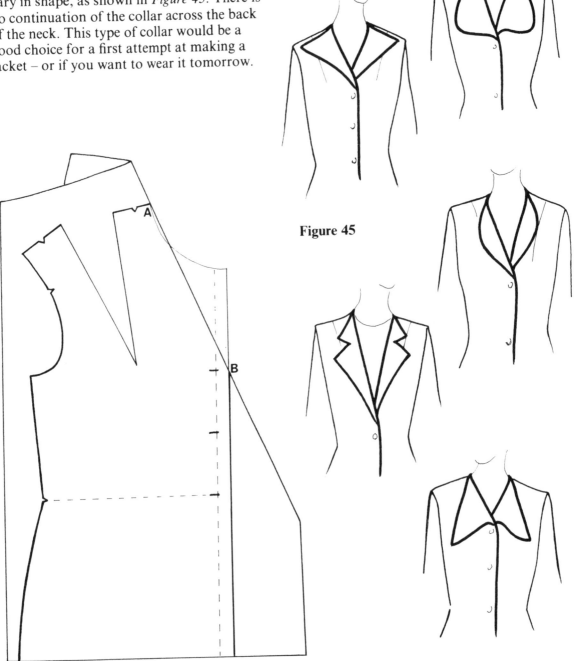

Figure 45

Figure 46

1 Rule a line from the neck point, **A**, to the front edge of the pattern at top-button level, **B** (*Figure 46*). Crease the pattern along this line and fold under.

2 On the bodice, between **A** and **B**, draw in the chosen outline of the revers (*Figure 47*).

3 Mark this outline, heavily, with the tracing wheel. Unfold the pattern; the perforations will give the outline of the revers (*Figure 48*). Make notch at **A**.

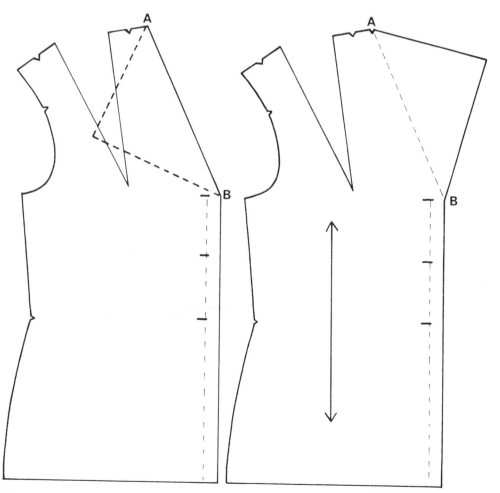

Figure 47   **Figure 48**

4 That was the underside of the revers; you have now to draft the facings which form the top layer and which finish the front edges. To allow for the thickness of fabric over the fold, and to prevent the edges of the revers from curling up, the facing must be cut wider. So place the pattern over a fresh sheet of paper, and trace round its whole outline, drawing the revers edges 0·3–0·5 cm outside the previous line, as shown in *Figure 49*.

5 Draw the inner edge of the facing, from C (5 cm to the left of A), widening to 10 cm down the front to D.

6 Cut out. Then cut down the inner edge of the facing (C–D). The right-hand section is the facing pattern, and the left-hand section becomes the pattern for the front lining (*Figure 50*).

7 Draft a back neck facing from the back pattern in the same way. Make this 5 cm wide from the centre-back A round to the shoulder seam B, to match the width of the front facing (*Figure 51*). Cut from A to B. The upper section is the back neck facing and the lower section, with the addition of 1 cm for a pleat down the centre-back, is the lining back pattern.

8 Mark straight-grain arrows on the front patterns, and fold arrows on the back patterns.

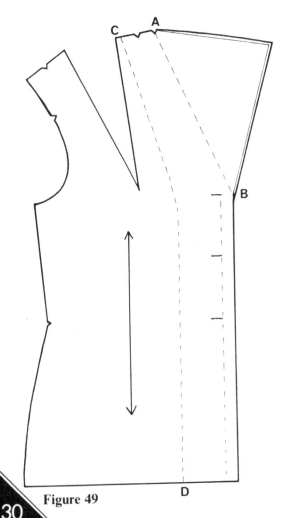

Figure 49

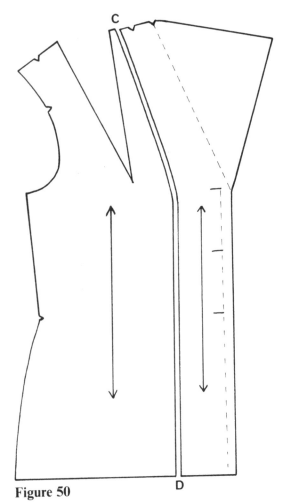

Figure 50

Rolled collar cut in one with revers

A rolled collar is one which stands up above the neckline seam, and rolls over to form revers.

The *stand* of the collar is the part above the neck seam; the *fall* is the part turned downwards; the *roll line* is the fold between the two. The *style-line* is the outer or free edge of the collar and revers.

Rolled collars can have any style-line. They may be shawl-shaped, as in the centre sketch in *Figure 52*, or they may be notched deeply or shallowly. Because there is no seam between the top-collar and the revers, the whole length of the collar and front facing is cut in one piece. In this pattern, there is a centre-back seam; you could dispense with this, but the pattern would then become very extravagant in its use of fabric, and the lower ends of the facings would be off-grain.

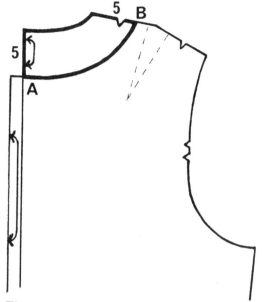

Figure 51

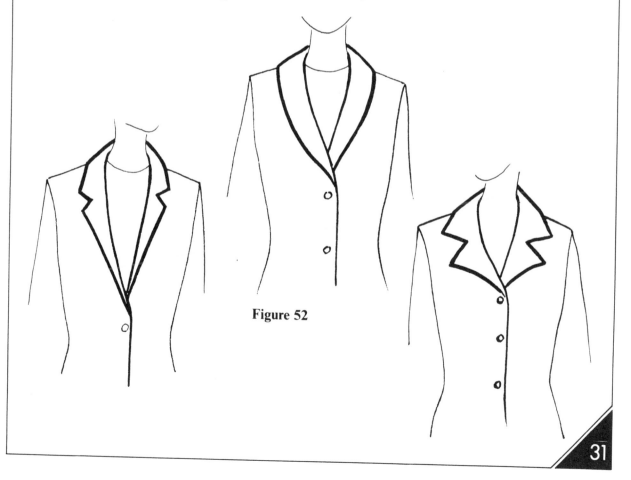

Figure 52

DESIGNING THE PATTERN

1 As before, trace round the front pattern; mark in the level of the top buttonhole, B, and the button-stand width (*Figure 44*).

2 Extend the shoulder line 2 cm to the right of the neck point A, and mark C. Rule a line from B through C and extend it 10 cm above C (*Figure 53*). This line represents the roll line.

3 Take the back pattern, *wrong* side up, and match its neck point to the neck point of the front pattern, A. For a collar with a high stand (about 3 cm) the centre-back of the pattern, D, should be 2 cm to the left of the line through C. (If you want a collar with a lower stand, to lie flatter round the back of the neck, then swing the back pattern further round, to *increase* the distance between D and the line running up from C. A distance of 3 cm will give a reduced stand of about 2 cm.)

4 Draw in the back neck curve from A to D. Draw in also about 10 cm down the centre-back line. Remove the back pattern (*Figure 54*).

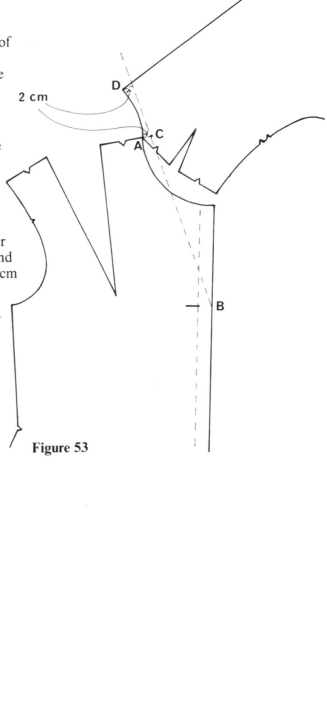

Figure 53

Figure 54

5 The fall of the collar must be wider than the stand, to cover the seamline at the back of the neck. Assuming a 3 cm stand, the fall should be 4–6 cm. Measure 3 cm for the stand from D to E.

6 Draw in the style-line on the bodice, measuring back from C to F on the shoulder line, for the width of the fall over the shoulder. Fold the pattern (as in *Figure 46*) along B–C, and trace with the wheel through both thicknesses the style-line of collar and revers from F down to B. Unfold the pattern (*Figure 55*) and mark in the outline of collar and revers from B to G.

7 Complete the style-line round the back of the collar from G to H, joining the line D–E at right angles, so that there will be a straight line across the back of the collar. Cut out the pattern for the jacket front and under collar.

8 For the top-collar and facing, trace round the whole front pattern on fresh paper. Draw the collar and revers edges 0·3–0·5 cm outside the previous outline, so that the top collar is slightly deeper than the under-collar (*Figure 56*).

9 Draw the inner edge of the facing from J, 5 cm to the left of A, widening to 10 cm down the front to K.

10 Cut out the pattern. Then cut from J to K. The right-hand section is the top-collar and facing; the left-hand section becomes the pattern for the front lining. Mark in straight-grain arrows.

11 Draft a back-neck facing and back lining as in *Figure 51*, and mark fold arrows.

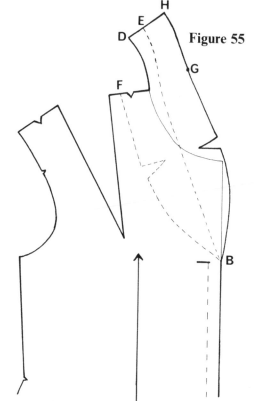

Figure 55

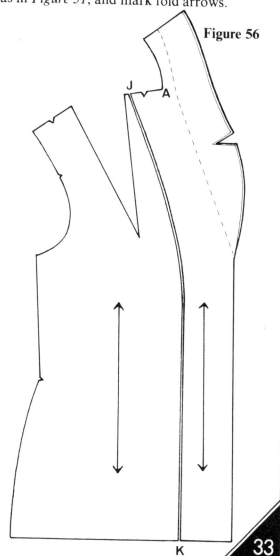

Figure 56

Rolled collar cut separately from revers
Figure 57 and the photograph on page 20 show this classic collar, which is seamed to the jacket round the neckline. The top-collar is usually cut on the straight-grain, and has no centre-back seam. The under-collar always has a centre-back seam and is always cut on the cross to settle smoothly under the roll. The collar fits closely to the back of the neck, so it is cut slightly narrower than the previous collar.

1 On fresh paper, draw round the jacket front pattern as you have developed it so far (*Figure 58*). Mark A at the neck point. Add a button-stand of 2 cm and mark B at the top-buttonhole level.

2 Draw in a new neckline dropping at the front 2 cm below the original one. Mark C.

3 Extend the shoulderline 2 cm from A to D.

4 Rule a line from B, up through D. Mark E where this crosses the neckline.

5 Measure the neckline of the jacket *back* pattern, and mark that length from D up to F.

6 Through F, draw a line at right angles to the line B–F.

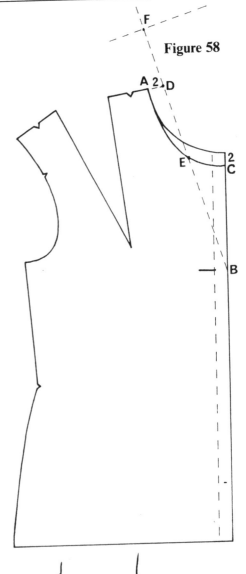

Figure 58

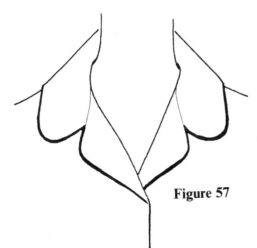

Figure 57

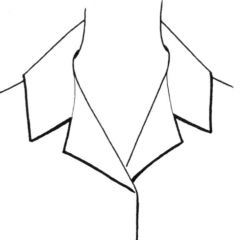

7 *Figure 59* G is 2 cm to the left of F. Join G–A. (G–A is the back neckline of the collar; G–F is the height of the stand.)

8 Crease the pattern from B to F, and fold under the *left-hand* part of the pattern. With the tracing wheel, mark the line E–C through to the bodice. Unfold the pattern. Mark H to correspond to C.

9 *Figure 60* Draw in the collar and revers on the bodice, from J (4 cm to the left of A) down to B. H–K and H–L should be the same length, about 4 cm. H–L is drawn as a continuation of E–H.

10 *Figure 61* Crease the pattern again from B to F, and fold under the *right-hand* part of the pattern. Trace with the wheel the final outline of collar and revers from J–K–H–L–B, through to M–N–C–P–B.

11 Draw a slightly curved line from M, to meet at a right angle the extended line from F. Mark Q. That completes the under-collar.

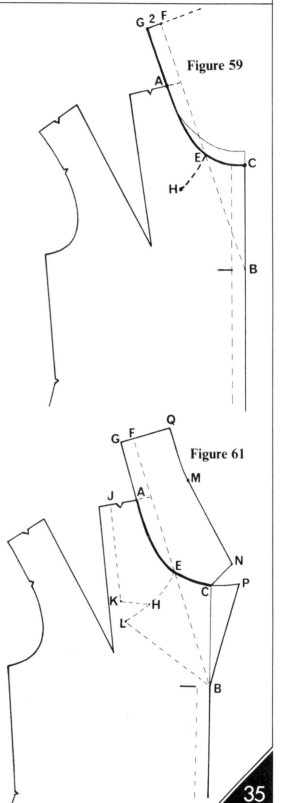

Figure 59

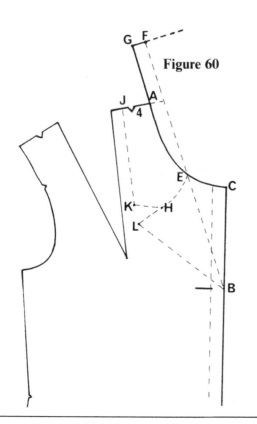

Figure 60

Figure 61

12 *Figure 62* Cut along the line A–E–C to separate the under-collar from the jacket front. Mark in a straight-grain arrow on the collar piece, diagonally to the centre-back G–Q. Mark a notch on the collar at A, on the jacket at C, and on both at E.

13 *Figure 63* For the top-collar, draw round the under-collar pattern and add 0·3 cm (or up to 0·5 cm for a thick tweed) along the edges Q–N and N–C. Mark the same notches, and put in a fold arrow at the centre-back.

14 *Figure 64* For the front facing, on fresh paper draw round the jacket front pattern. Draw the outline of the revers 0·3–0·5 cm outside C–P and P–B. Draw the inner edge of the facing from 5 cm to the left of A, widening to 10 cm down the front to the hemline. Cut along this line to separate the front facing pattern from the remainder, which becomes the front lining pattern. Mark in straight-grain arrows.

15 Draft a back neck facing and back lining as in *Figure 51*, and mark fold arrows.

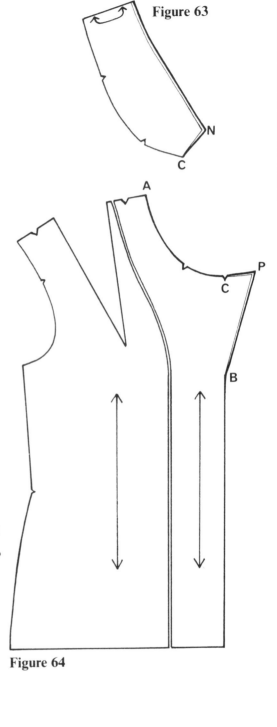

Figure 63

Figure 64

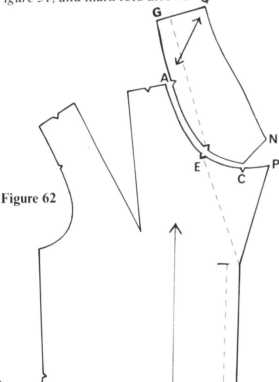

Figure 62

THE LENGTH

The jacket blocks are cut to hip depth, but if you want a shorter line simply rule across and cut the pattern to the length required.

Jacket with a peplum *Figure 65*

1 Trace round the block to the length required. You may wish to fit the waist more closely by widening the darts.

2 Add the width of the button-stand. You may like to round off the corners at the hemline.

3 Draft the front facing as in *Figures 49* and *50*.

4 Cut along the waistline to separate the peplum from the jacket. (Do not cut the facing pattern.)

5 Cut the peplum into sections as shown in *Figure 66*. Spread apart their lower edges, and draw round them for the new flared outline. Mark a straight-grain arrow parallel to the front edge.

6 Draft a back peplum pattern from the back block in the same way. Mark a fold arrow at centre-back.

Jacket with a drawstring waist

For a waist finish like the jacket on page 10 trace round the block allowing 5 cm below the waistline (or more if you wish) for blousing. Draw the side seam straight, and omit any waist dart shaping (*Figure 67*).

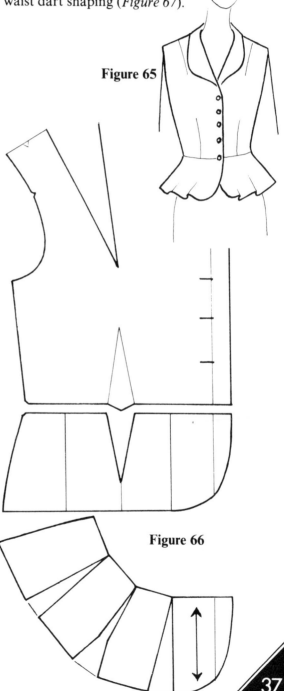

Figure 65

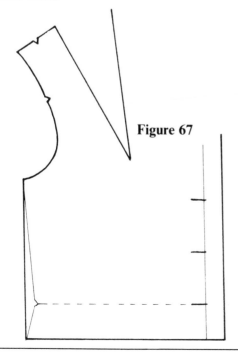

Figure 67

Figure 66

THE SLEEVES

The unaltered sleeve block will give an easy-fitting sleeve suitable for worsted, tweed or any thick fabric. It was the pattern used for the jacket on page 20.

In a thinner fabric a more fitted sleeve might be wanted. This could be cut narrower either from just below the armhole or from below the elbow, using dart shaping. The sleeve must, though, be wide enough to allow 5 cm ease round the upper arm, both for movement and for any sweater sleeve. At the elbow, it should not be less than about 32 cm, and at the wrist not less than 23 cm, to slip easily over your hand.

In jersey, the stretch of the material makes possible a tighter sleeve; the jacket on page 23, of cotton jersey and unlined, has only 2 cm ease at the elbow – but this style would be worn over a blouse only.

Semi-fitted sleeves *Figure 68*
The width of the sleeve above the elbow can be kept unaltered, while an elbow dart reduces the forearm and cuff measurement.

1 Draw round the sleeve block. Mark in the centre line, the back arm line and the line P–Q.

2 Cut up the lines from the wrist to just short of P–Q, and then cut from P to Q (*Figure 69*).

3 Overlap the sections until you have tightened the wrist to the measurement you want. This will open up an elbow dart (*Figure 70*).

4 Draw round the pattern on fresh paper, marking in the dart. Shorten the dart to the back arm line, to give more room over the elbow.

5 If the dart is more than 4 cm wide, it will tend to poke at the point. To avoid this, draw in two darts instead of one, dividing the width equally between them, and leaving a space of 2 cm between them.

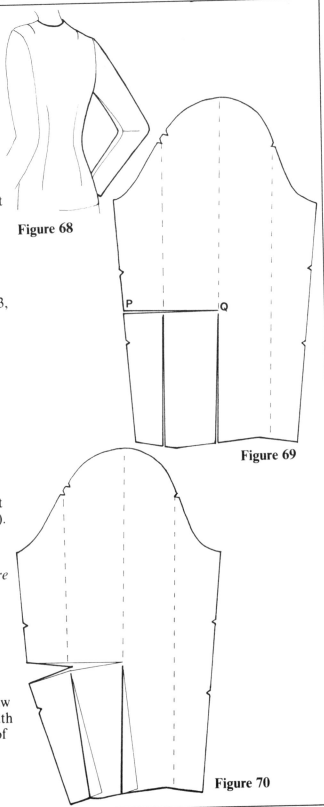

Figure 68

Figure 69

Figure 70

6 Fold in the darts, as shown in *Figures 6–8*. Mark across their ends with the tracing wheel and unfold. This gives the shaping of the seamline (*Figure 71*).

Narrowed sleeves
Without an elbow dart, the pattern can be cut narrower from just below the armhole. The sides of the sleeve may be straight *or* curved inwards, according to the effect you want (*Figure 72*).

Flared sleeves   *Figure 73*
A sleeve flared at the forearm may look more effective if the upper arm is tightened. The development of this pattern is shown in the photographs on page 22, and the finished style on page 23.

A sleeve can also be flared from the shoulder, as in *Figure 74*; but unless it is taken into a cuff it could look shapeless.

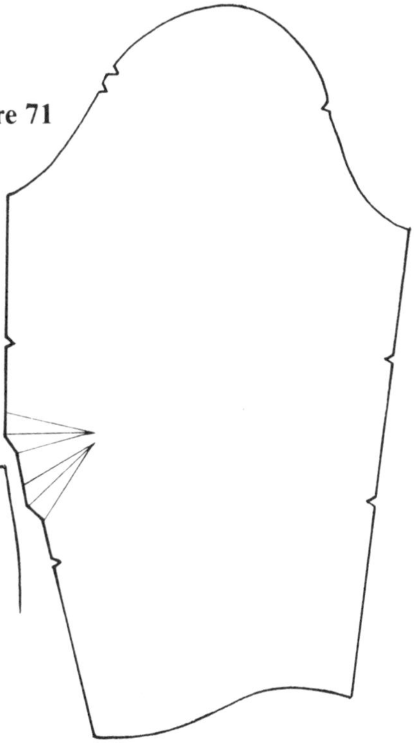

Figure 71

Figure 73

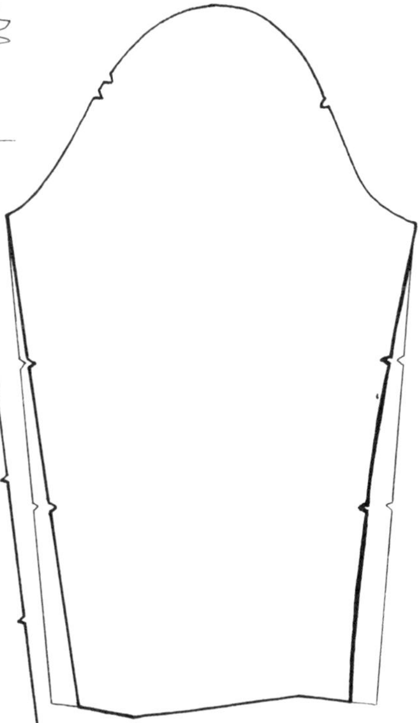

Figure 72

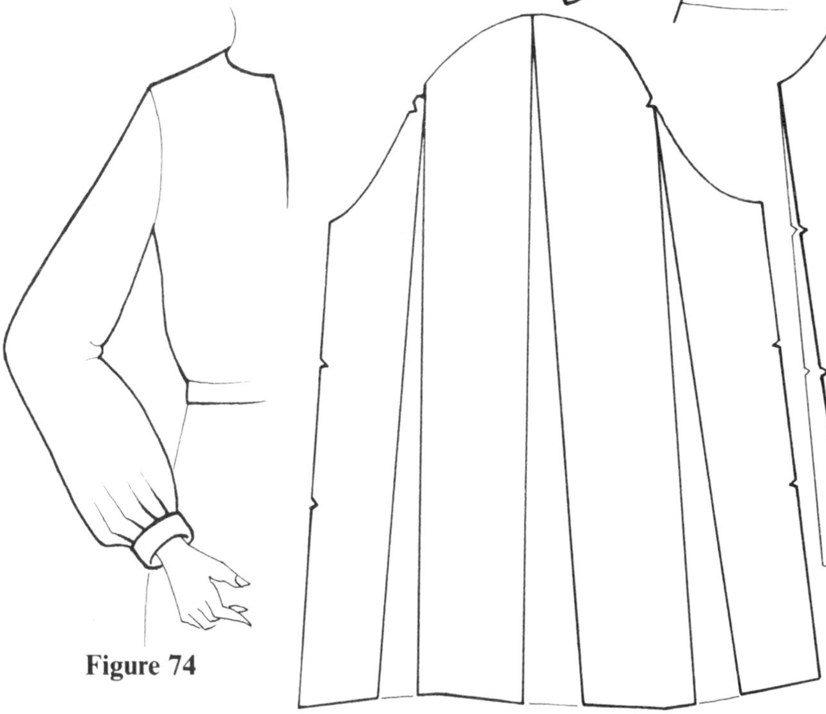

Figure 74

Full-crowned sleeves *Figure 75*
By cutting and spreading the pattern, width or height can be introduced at the shoulder. A pleated sleevehead should be planned with wide shoulder-pads, which will affect the cut of the bodice shoulderline. The pattern is developed as shown (for a short sleeve) in the photograph on page 47. The sections of the sleevehead are there raised 5 cm at the centre, and the darts are 3 cm wide.

The silhouette of this sleevehead depends entirely on the length of the darts. If stitched very short, they will force the material upwards at the point of the dart; the longer the darts are stitched, the more horizontal the crown of the sleeve will be. The darts may be stitched for their full length or only part-way, as dart-tucks. It is advisable to cut a trial sleeve from old sheeting, as the finished effect is very difficult to gauge on paper.

A gathered sleeve is possible, but may be clumsy on a jacket; the pattern would be cut and spread apart as shown in *Figure 76*.

Cuffs *Figure 77*
The simplest cuff is just an extension of the sleeve, folded back. Fold the lower edge of the pattern paper and crease along the required depth of the cuff, perhaps 5–7 cm. Crease again at the same depth (*Figure 78*). Place the lower corners of the sleeve block (ignoring the wristline shaping) to the folded edge of the paper, trace round, cut and unfold.

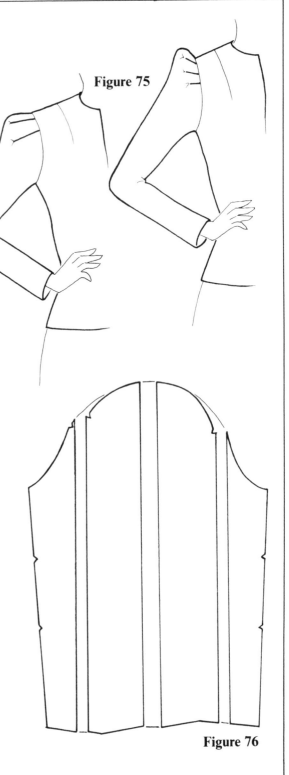

Figure 75

Figure 76

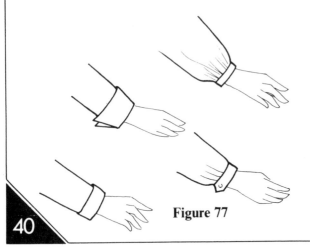

Figure 77

A separate turn-back cuff and facing can be cut with square or pointed corners. Draw it the length of the sleeve wristline and double the finished depth, plus 3 cm as a facing inside the sleeve (*Figure 79*).

A separate cuff-band is a good finish for a gathered or pleated sleeve, as in the jacket on page 10. This is drafted double, as a wide band below a sleeve opening, so you will need an overlap of 3 cm, marked with a notch (*Figure 80*). Mark the sleeve opening 6–8 cm up the back armline of the sleeve.

With no sleeve opening, the band is seamed into a circle – which must be drafted big enough to let your hand pass through easily.

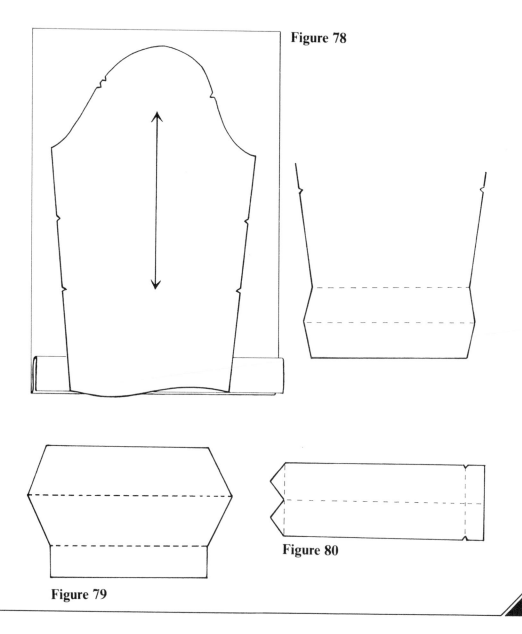

Figure 78

Figure 79

Figure 80

POCKETS *Figure 81*

The kinds of pocket, their placing and their proportion are of immense importance to the design, as they are so conspicuous. It is much easier to judge the effect on the figure than on paper; if you made a mock-up jacket from sheeting when fitting the blocks, try it on now and mark on it the line for a bound pocket or the shape of a patch pocket. Then transfer the markings to the jacket front pattern.

In the following patterns, seam allowances are included.

Patch pockets

Plain rectangular patch pockets, such as the ones photographed on page 10, are the easiest of all pockets to make.

1 Draw the finished shape of the pocket.

2 Add 3 cm along the top edge, for the facing and seam allowance. Add 1·5 cm along the other edges (*Figure 82*).

3 For the lining, add nothing to the top edge, but 1·5 cm along the others. The lining seam will fall 1·5 cm inside the pocket opening.

Pocket detail of the jacket shown on page 20

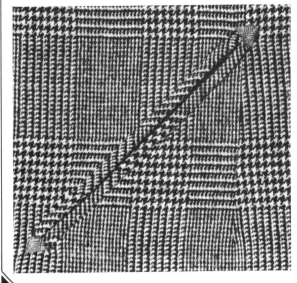

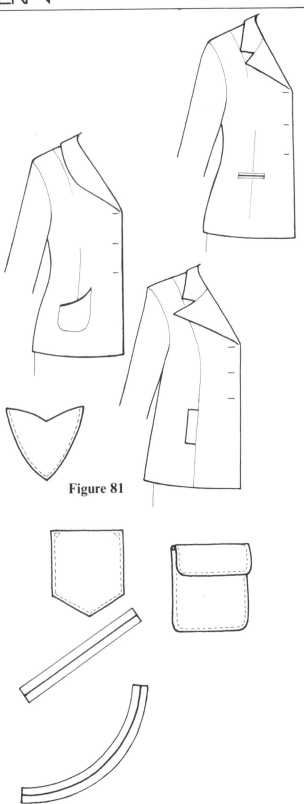

Figure 81

Patch pocket with a flap

Add twice the depth of the flap to the length of the pocket piece; then add 3 cm for the facing and seam allowance. Add 1·5 cm along the other edges (*Figure 83*). The lining is cut as above.

Patch pocket with shaped opening

The two pockets at the upper left of *Figure 81*, and any other shapes where the pocket mouth is not cut straight, will need a seam along the opening. Both pocket and lining are therefore drafted the finished size, both with 1·5 cm seam allowances added all round.

Welted pockets

This type of pocket is best set into a side-front seam as in the centre sketch in *Figure 81*. (See page 24 for adding seams.)

1 Mark the pocket position and length with a pair of notches on the seamline.

2 Draft the welt twice its finished width, by the length of the pocket opening between the notches. Add 1·5 cm seam allowances all round (*Figure 84*).

3 The pocket bag is cut – in lining fabric – to the depth of the pocket opening (A–B) plus 10 cm; the width is 15 cm. Shape as shown in *Figure 85*. Add 1·5 cm seam allowances all round.

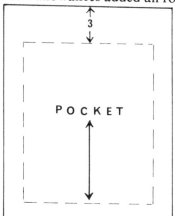

3

Figure 82

POCKET

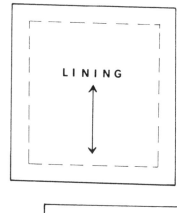

LINING

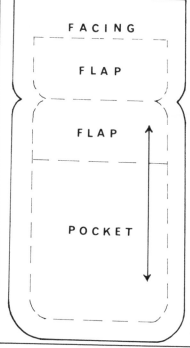

FACING

FLAP

FLAP

POCKET

Figure 83

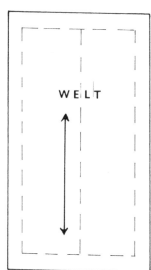

WELT

Figure 84

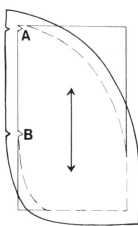

A

B

Figure 85

Bound pockets

The top right-hand sketch in *Figure 81* shows a plain bound pocket. In the jacket on page 20 (detail on page 42), the opening is slanted. All bound pockets need accurate workmanship and are rather more difficult to make than the previous types. If you are in doubt, try a plain horizontal bound pocket first; a sloping or curved pocket mouth is more complicated.

1 Draw the line of the pocket mouth on the jacket front. It should be wide enough for your hand, plus 2 cm. A much wider pocket may tend to gape. Above and below the opening, draw the width of the binding – about 0·6–0·8 cm.

2 Below the pocket marking, draw in the finished shape of the pocket bag. This must be shallow enough to be clear of the lining at the jacket hem. *Figure 86.*

3 The whole of the pocket may be made from the jacket fabric, or the lower half of the front may be replaced by lining material to reduce the bulk of a thick fabric.

4 *Figure 87* Draft the pocket:
Twice the depth of the pocket bag, plus
six times the depth of the binding, plus
3 cm for seam allowances
– say a total of 25 cm.

The *width* is the width of the pocket opening, plus 3 cm.

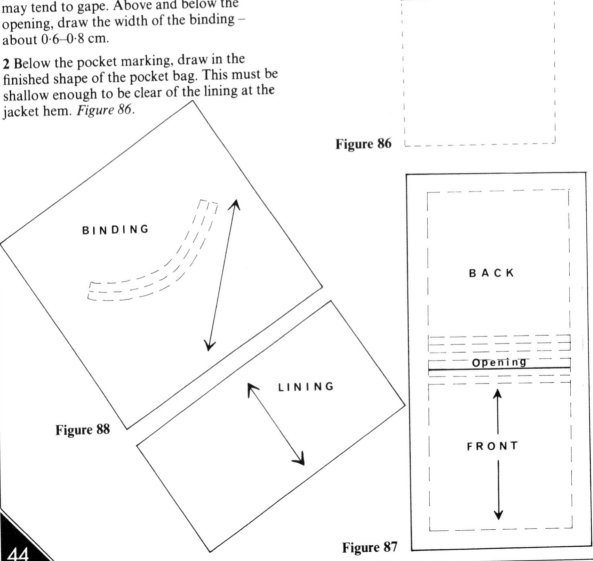

Figure 86

Figure 88

BINDING

LINING

BACK

Opening

FRONT

Figure 87

Bound pockets with curved or slanting openings
Draft the pocket binding on the true cross. It should be the width of the pocket opening plus 3 cm, and should be long enough to leave 10 cm clear, above and below the opening. *Figure 88* Both the back and front of the pocket, below the binding, should be cut from lining fabric; width as before, depth as required, plus two seam allowances.

THE LINING

Linings are cut 4 cm shorter at the hem, but otherwise to the same pattern as their corresponding jacket pieces, and made up with the same dart shaping. A pleat for ease is allowed down the back.

The lining pattern for the front, as far as the facings, is shown in *Figure 50*; and for the back in *Figure 51*.

SEAM AND HEM ALLOWANCES

Apart from the pockets, all the pattern pieces have been drafted 'net', without any turnings so far. Their edges all coincide with seamlines or with the length of a finished edge. Now, with all the drafting finished, is the time to add seam and hem allowances. The photographs on this and next page show the progression from blocks to patterns, and how these allowances are added to bring the patterns to their final state.

1 Add 1·5 cm to:
all seamlines, including wrist edges where there is a separate cuff;
all the edges of facings, collar, yoke and cuff;
the sides of dart markings. (Make sure you have first shortened the bust and sleeve darts, as in *Figures 36* and *70*).

2 Add 4 cm to the hem and wrist edges. In a thick fabric, a drawstring waist needs 5 cm.

3 Make the same additions to the lining pieces.

Draw or rule at these distances outside all the pattern outlines, and cut out. Check that the names of the pieces, the straight-grain lines or fold arrows, and the notches, are marked

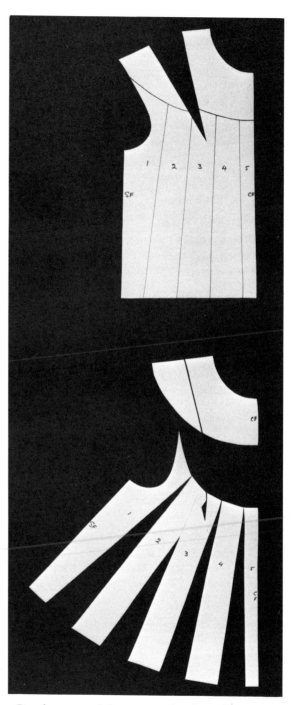

Development of the pattern for the jacket shown on page 23 – front and yoke

The patterns are now ready for laying out on the fabric.

FABRIC REQUIREMENTS

As you are not working with a commercial pattern, you will not have the guidance, on the envelope, as to the length of fabric needed.

So first choose your fabric, note its width and also any check or one-way design that may have to be matched. Next, make a pattern layout to see how much material you will need to buy. Only then should you buy.

The pattern layout

Unless you have a really large table, plan the layout of the pattern pieces on the floor.

1 Take the width of the fabric when folded in half, with the selvages matched. Use the edge of a carpet to represent the fold of the fabric, and a long ruler or straight edge, placed parallel to it and the appropriate distance away, to represent the selvage edges.

2 Place your pattern pieces, as economically as possible, with the straight-grain arrows parallel to the edges, and the fold arrows placed to the fold. *Figure 89* shows a typical layout; place the larger pieces first, and the smaller ones where they will fit.

3 As your fabric will be folded, you will automatically cut two of each piece. But if you are having separately-faced cuffs, you will need four pieces; so the cuff pattern will need to be laid twice.

4 If you have chosen a fabric with a one-way surface texture or nap, or with any design that will not reverse, then all the pattern pieces must be laid with their tops towards the same end of the layout.

5 If the fabric is checked, add two complete repeats of the check to the measured length of your layout, to allow for precise matching.

The fabric and notions

Only now are you ready to buy the right length of fabric and lining. At the same time, buy what Americans call the 'notions' – the

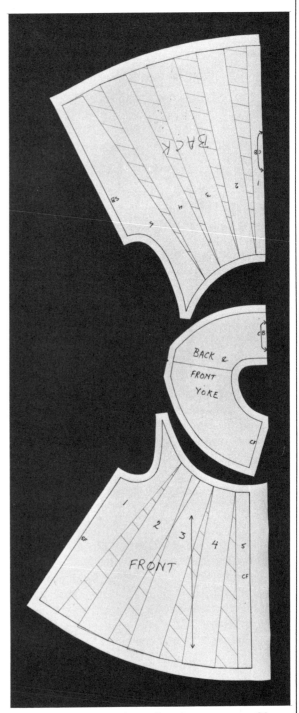

The final pattern for the jacket shown on page 23

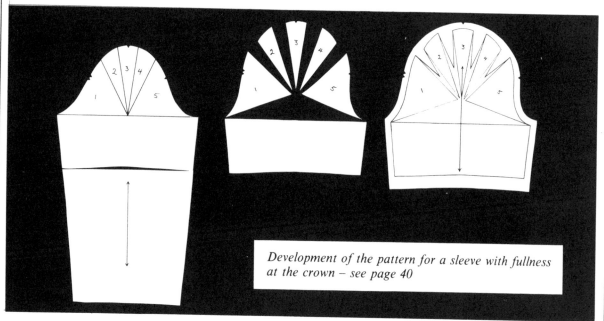

Development of the pattern for a sleeve with fullness at the crown – see page 40

bits and pieces to make up the jacket:
matching thread;
buttonhole twist for top-stitching, or for hand-worked buttonholes;
buttons.

The interfacing

Use either fusible woven interfacing, or the non-woven trellis-cut type. Both are ironed on with steam, and both have enough 'give' to avoid leaving an ugly line at the edge of a front facing, and for a collar to set smoothly.

You will need interfacing cut to patterns of:
the front facing (excluding the hem);
the back neck facing;
the under-collar;
the patch pocket (or, in firm fabric, for the top edge only);
the pocket welt (half width);
the cuff.

You will also need enough interfacing to cut strips for the jacket hem edge, and for wrist edges where there is no cuff.

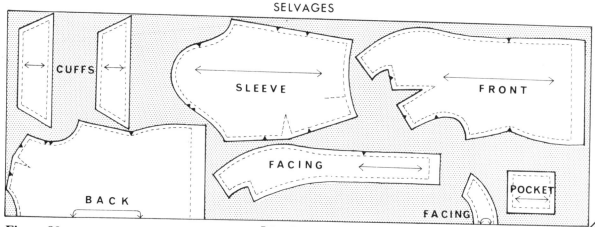

Figure 89

The instructions that follow give the order in which you should work, whatever type of jacket you are making. As you go along, *pick out the instructions for your particular design and disregard the rest.*

The instructions are for straightforward dressmaker's methods, and do not include any tailoring.

CUTTING OUT

Fold the fabric lengthwise, with the right side inside. It is important that the selvages (or stripes of a patterned material) should be perfectly matched, so that the fold is exactly on the straight grain of the fabric. Press the material with steam, if necessary, to get rid of any distortion.

Place the pattern pieces in the positions you have planned, with their straight-grain arrows parallel to the selvages. A fold arrow goes precisely to the fold, not a millimetre or two away from it. With a checked fabric, the most conspicuous line – or the centre of the space between checks – should come at the centre-front and back. The check should be symmetrical on the collar, and should correspond at the back to the jacket checks.

Smooth the pieces down their centres, hold them with one pin at each end, check the straight-grain arrow again, and then smooth out and pin down the corners. Finally, pin all round the piece at intervals of 10 to 15 cm.

When you cut out, notches should be cut outwards, not into the seam allowance. Leave the patterns pinned to the jacket pieces.

Cut linings to correspond to the back and front (as far as the facings) and to the sleeve – also to pockets if necessary.

Cut interfacings to correspond to all facings, and on the same grain.

MARKING

The patterns already have their seam allowances marked round the fitting lines. It is extremely important that your seams be stitched precisely along these lines, or the fit will be affected. So mark the vital points, through the pattern on to the fabric, as a guide for your machining. There are several ways to do this.

Dressmaker's carbon paper

Insert the carbon paper (face downwards) between the pattern and the upper layer of fabric; place another carbon (face upwards) under the lower layer. On a firm surface, mark through the pattern with the tracing wheel, making a cross at the point to be marked. The marks will be transferred to the wrong side of the fabric.

Tailor's tacks

This method is nearly as quick and rather more reliable, since carbon markings may not show up well on rough-surfaced woollen materials.

1 Using a double thread, take a tiny stitch through the pattern and both thicknesses of fabric, at the point to be marked (*Figure 90*).

2 Take another stitch through the same point, and leave a loop big enough to put your finger through (*Figure 91*).

3 Cut the thread, leaving 1 cm ends (*Figure 92*).

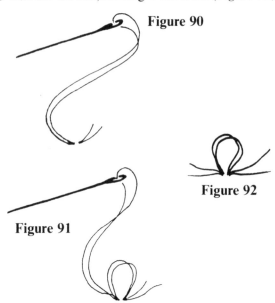

Figure 90

Figure 92

Figure 91

4 When you have marked all the points on the pattern piece, gently tear off the pattern. If your stitches were small, so will the holes be.   Then ease apart the two layers of fabric and cut the threads between them (*Figure 93*).

5 You will be left with tufts of thread in each piece of fabric, which can be matched with their opposite numbers when you pin the seams.

Points to be marked

1 The points where seamlines cross, such as the ends of a yoke and the underarm points of bodice and sleeve.

2 Dart markings, at the point, sides and seamline.

3 The centre of the sleevehead.

4 The corners of collar and revers.

5 The neck-point of a collar cut in one with facings (A, *Figure 56*).

6 The corners of patch pocket placings.

7 The line of a bound pocket, on the jacket and on the pocket piece.

8 The positions of buttons and buttonholes.

INTERFACING

Trim off the seam allowances of the interfacing pieces. Using steam, press the interfacing to the wrong side of the under-collar, jacket fronts and back neckline. Interface the cuffs and pocket welts as far as the fold. Interface the whole of patch pockets, or the top 3 cm only, according to the firmness of the fabric.

DARTS

Stitch the shoulder and any waist darts, from the wide end to the point. The point should be finely tapered off (*Figure 94*). Cut open down the centre of the dart, and press the sides apart. Clip seam allowances at the centre of waist darts.

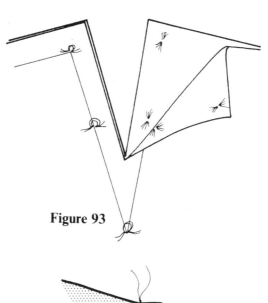

Figure 93

Figure 94

YOKES

1 Gather or pleat the bodice sections to fit the yokes.

2 Stitch the yoke seams and press the turnings upwards.

3 Trim the turnings in layers, to different widths, to avoid bulk above the seam (*Figure 95*).

4 If liked, top-stitch with buttonhole twist and the longest machine stitch, 1 cm above the seamline.

5 For a pleat below a back yoke, tack the whole length of the pleat in place before stitching the seam (*Figure 96*).

SIDE-FRONT SEAMS WITH WELTED POCKETS

1 Make up the welt first by stitching the short seam at each end. Trim the turnings into layers, turn right side out and press. Top-stitch if liked (*Figure 97*).

2 With right sides together, tack the welt to the jacket front, between the notches (*Figure 98*).

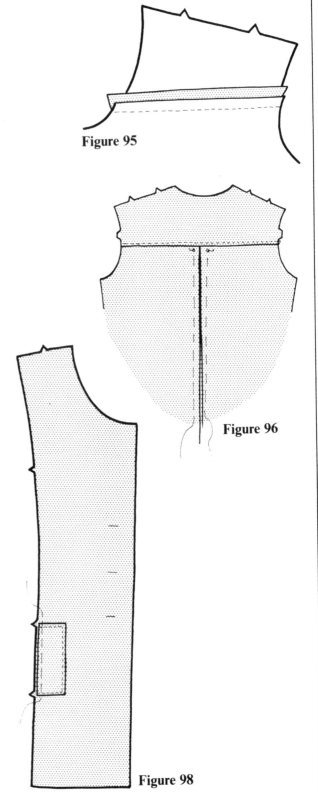

Figure 95

Figure 96

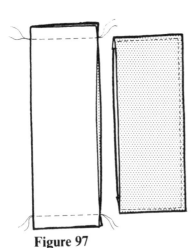

Figure 97

Figure 98

3 With right sides together, tack and stitch one pocket piece to the jacket front, over the welt. Tack and stitch the other pocket piece to the jacket side-front between the notches (*Figure 99*).

4 With right sides together, stitch the side-front seam. Pivot at the top of the pocket opening, stitch round the pocket bag, pivot at the bottom of the pocket opening, and stitch the rest of the seam (*Figure 100*).

5 Clip the seam turnings of the side-front into the corners of the seam (*Figure 101*). Press the seam open, with the pocket pressed towards the front and the welt towards the side. From the inside of the jacket, back-stitch the ends of the welt to the side-front.

6 Side-front seams without pocket openings should also be stitched at this stage.

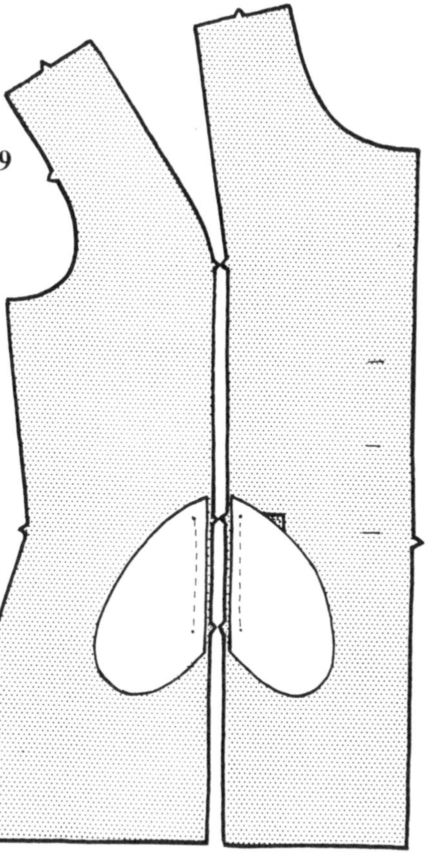

Figure 99

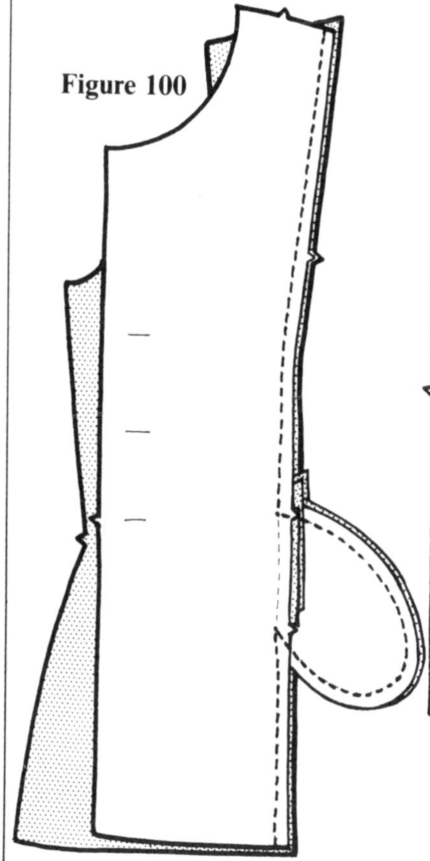

Figure 100

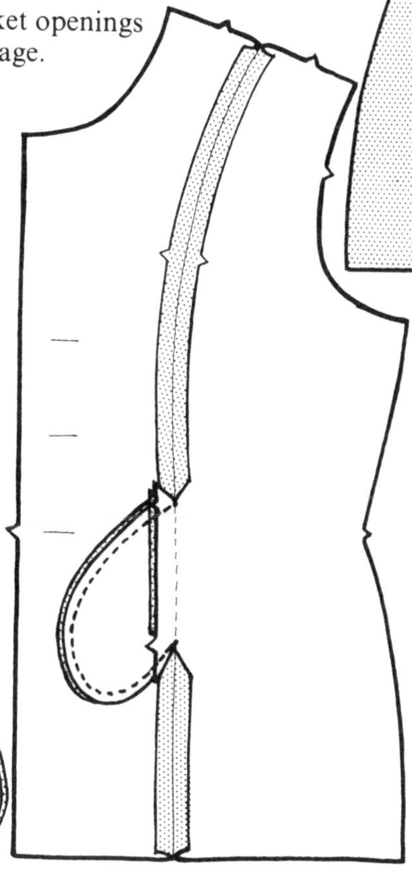

Figure 101

51

PLAIN PATCH POCKETS

1 Press 3 cm along the pocket top to the right side. Press the 1·5 cm seam allowance at the top of the pocket lining to the wrong side (*Figure 102*).

2 Place pocket and lining right sides together as shown in *Figure 103*. Stitch the seam round the pocket. Trim the corners.

3 Turn right side out through the opening at the top of the lining. Slip-hem the top fold of the lining to the pocket.

PATCH POCKETS WITH FLAPS

Press half the depth of the flap, above the shaping, to the right side (*Figure 104*). Then continue as above.

PATCH POCKETS WITH SHAPED OPENINGS

Match pocket and lining with right sides together and stitch all round, leaving a small opening at the side. Trim corners, clip curves, turn right-side out and press (*Figure 105*).

ATTACHING PATCH POCKETS

1 Strengthen the top of the pocket position by pinning a piece of tape or a strip of lining fabric to the wrong side of the jacket front, between the top corner markings for the pocket.

2 Tack the pocket in place and top-stitch close to its side and lower edges, beginning and ending with a small square or triangle of stitching (*Figure 106*).

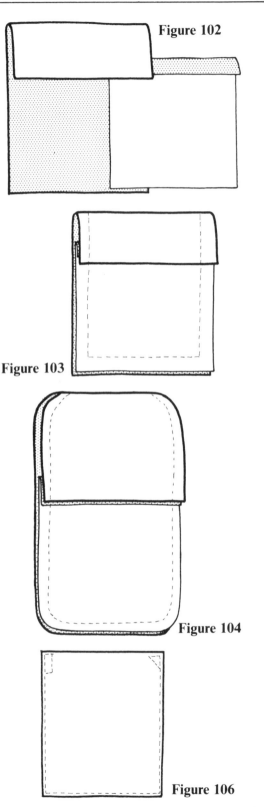

Figure 102

Figure 103

Figure 104

Figure 105

Figure 106

BOUND POCKETS

1 Press a strip of interfacing to the wrong side of the jacket front, behind the pocket placing.

2 With right sides together, tack the pocket to the jacket front, matching the pocket markings.

3 Stitch above and below the pocket marking, and across its ends, as one continuous seam. Pivot at the corners and overlap the last few stitches over the first (*Figure 107*). The distance of the stitching from the pocket marking, 0·6–0·8 cm, will be the finished width of the binding. The stitching at the ends should run exactly across the ends of the pocket opening.

4 Cut through both thicknesses along the pocket marking, and snip into the corners (*Figure 108*).

5 Turn the pocket through to the wrong side. Press the two lips of the pocket to meet at the centre of the slit, and press the turnings at each end outwards from the pocket to form pleats (*Figure 109*).

6 Stab-stitch all round the pocket, on the seamline, to secure the binding above and below the opening (*Figure 110*).

7 Press the back of the pocket down to match its edges to the pocket front. Fold the jacket out of the way and stitch round the pocket bag as shown in *Figure 111*, beginning and ending at the ends of the pocket mouth.

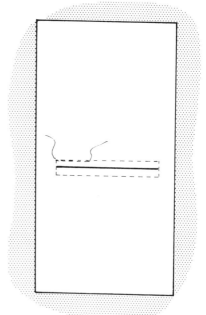

Figure 107

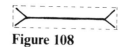

Figure 108

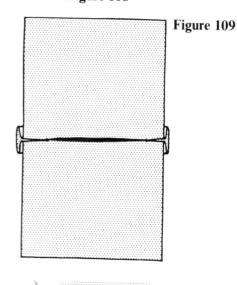

Figure 109

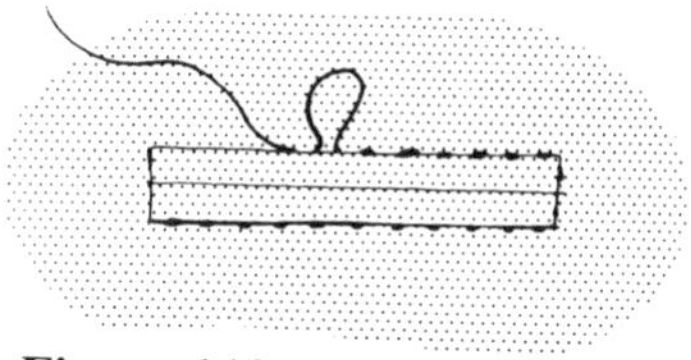

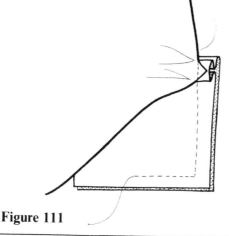

Figure 111

Figure 110

BOUND BUTTONHOLES: FIRST STAGE

Bound buttonholes are easier to make at this stage, when you are handling only the right front, not the whole jacket. They are made in very much the same way as bound pockets. They are not finished off, on the facing side, until the jacket is completed.

1 On the wrong (interfaced) side of the right front, mark in pencil the length of each buttonhole – 0·5 cm longer than the button. Between the end of the buttonhole and the edge of the fabric, there should be a button-stand of 2 cm or more, and a seam allowance of 1·5 cm. Be sure that the spaces between the buttonhole markings are identical.

2 Cut a fabric patch 8 cm square for the binding of each buttonhole. Matching the straight grain, tack it (right side down) to the outside of the jacket front, over the buttonhole placing.

3 Working from the wrong side (where you can see the marking), stitch round the buttonhole as in *Figure 112*, pivoting on the needle at the corners and working the last few stitches over the first few. The distance of the stitching above and below the buttonhole marking will make the width of the binding.

4 Cut the buttonhole open through all thicknesses. Clip right into each corner (*Figure 113*) to make little triangles at the ends.

5 Turn the patch through to the wrong side, pull the ends apart to form pleats, and press (*Figure 114*). On the right side, make sure that the binding meets precisely along the centre of the buttonhole (*Figure 115*).

6 Tack round the buttonhole through all thicknesses. From the right side, machine round all four sides, exactly along the seamline. This stitching will be invisible (*Figure 116*). (Yes, it *will* be; it will sink into the seam.)

7 Trim off any surplus binding. The facing of the buttonhole is done later.

Figure 112

Figure 113

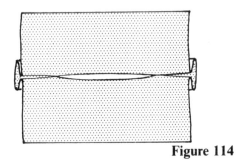

Figure 114

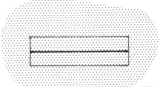

Figure 115

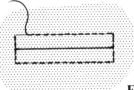

Figure 116

THE BODY SEAMS

1 Stitch any side-back seams.

2 Stitch peplum waist seams.

3 Stitch the shoulder seams. For a rolled collar cut in one with the revers, the jacket shoulder and neckline seams are worked across in one continuous operation. First, at centre-back, seam together the under-collar extensions. Then stitch the left shoulder seam; clip into the corner, pivot and continue round the back neckline; clip and pivot again, and stitch the right shoulder seam.

4 Stitch the side seams.

5 Press all seams open, and clip the seam allowances at any curves.

For a lined jacket, no other finishing of the seam turnings is needed. However, if you do not want a lining (for instance, on a loose jersey jacket such as that on page 23), then finish the seams in one of the two following ways.

i Top-stitch each side of the seam (*Figure 117*).

ii Trim the back turning to half its width. Press the front turning over it, and herringbone-stitch in place (*Figure 118*).

THE COLLAR AND FACINGS

For a simple revers front
With right sides together, stitch the back and front facings at the shoulder seams. Press the seams open (*Figure 119*).

For a rolled collar cut in one with the revers
1 Stitch the centre-back seam of the facings, press open and trim.

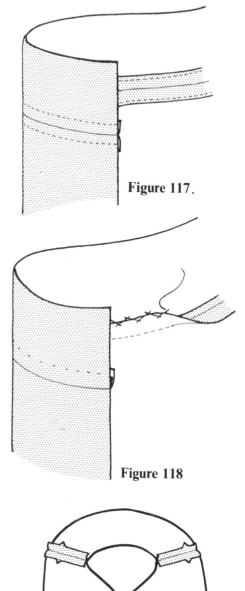

Figure 117.

Figure 118

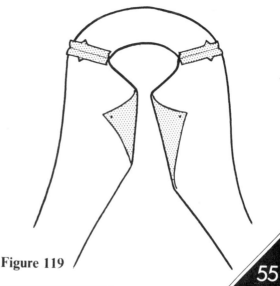

Figure 119

2 Strengthen the corners of the facing by machining in to the neck point marking as shown in *Figure 120*. Clip into the V shape.

3 Stitch the back neck facing to the front facings, pivoting on the needle at the corners (*Figure 121*). Clip and trim the turnings, and press open.

For a rolled collar cut separately from the revers

1 With right sides together, stitch the centre-back seam of the under-collar, press open and trim the turnings narrowly (*Figure 122*).

2 Overlap the centre-back edges of the interfacing, stitch the seam and trim the turnings (*Figure 123*).

3 Press the interfacing to the wrong side of the under-collar, using steam.

4 With right sides together, stitch the under-collar to the jacket, matching notches to shoulder seams. Begin and end the stitching at the corner marking of the collar; do not continue into the seam allowance (*Figure 124*).

5 Clip the turnings as shown and press the seam open.

6 Stitch the back neck facing to the front facings at the shoulders. Press seams open.

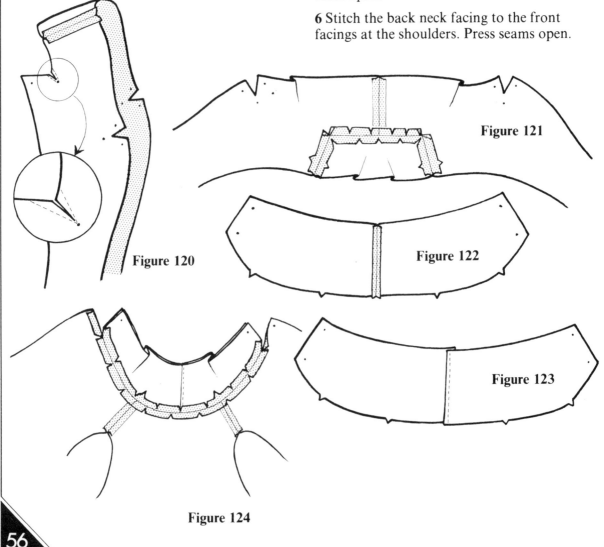

Figure 120

Figure 121

Figure 122

Figure 123

Figure 124

7 With right sides together, stitch the top-collar to the facings along the neckline, matching the notches to the shoulder seams. Clip the turnings as before and press the seam open (*Figure 125*).

ATTACHING THE FACINGS

1 With right sides together, tack the completed facings to the jacket. Stitch from the centre-back, round the edge of the collar and revers (pivoting at the step) and down one front to the hemline. Then stitch the other side (*Figure 126*).

2 Clip and trim the turnings in layers and fold the facings to the inside of the jacket. Roll the seam between your finger and thumb and press so that the seam falls a hair's breadth out of sight under the revers and round the collar or neckline.

3 Below top-button level, press the seam a hair's breadth to the inside; it should then be invisible when the jacket is being worn.

4 Tack the facings and collar in position, a couple of centimetres from the seamline.

5 Roll the collar over, as it will be worn, and tack it to the under-collar along the back neckline seams. Under the back facing, catch the seam turnings firmly together (*Figure 127*).

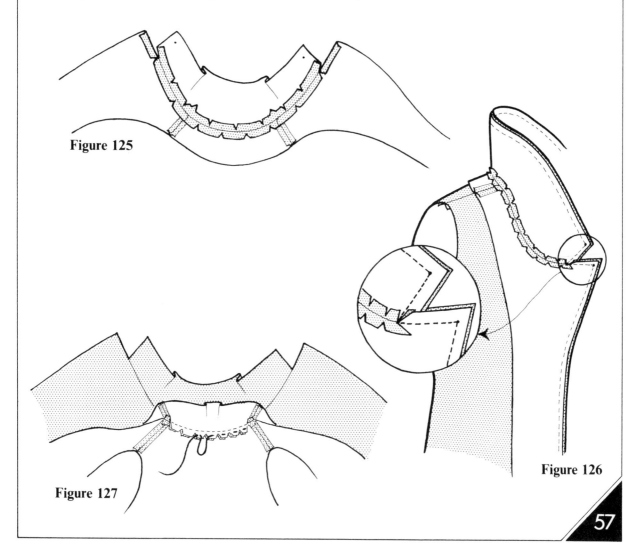

Figure 125

Figure 126

Figure 127

THE SLEEVES

Since you will already have fitted the jacket, the sleeve length will be right. So you can make up and finish the sleeve before setting it into the armhole. This way, it is much easier to handle.

The sleevehead should first be shaped in to fit the armhole. Even a fitted sleeve (such as the one on page 20) has 2–3 cm ease at the crown, and you must first dispose of this.

Gathers

Run two gathering threads (longest machine stitch) round the sleevehead between the notches, at 1 cm and 2 cm from the edge (*Figure 128*).

Darts

A full sleevehead such as *Figure 75* is darted as in *Figure 129*. Stitch also any elbow dart, and press downwards.

Interfacing

If the sleeve is to be finished without any cuff or band, cut a strip of interfacing 3 cm wide and press it to the wrong side of the sleeve above the hem allowance (*Figure 130*).

If the sleeve is to have an attached cuff, interface the upper half of the cuff extension (*Figure 131*).

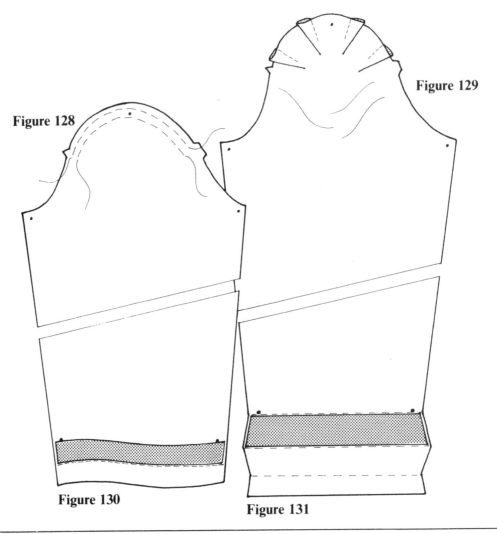

Figure 128

Figure 129

Figure 130

Figure 131

MAKING UP THE JACKET

The sleeve opening

1 Cut a facing 5 cm longer than the opening, and 8 cm wide.

2 Matching the straight grain, stitch the facing over the marking of the opening. At the wrist, the stitching should be 1 cm from the marking, tapering to a point at the apex. Work one stitch only across the point (*Figure 132*).

3 Cut up the marking. Turn and press the facing through to the wrong side (*Figure 133*).

The sleeve seam
Stitch and press open.

Plain wrist finish
Turn up, press and catch-stitch the hem (*Figure 134*).

Attached fold-back cuffs
Turn the sleeve inside out. Press half the depth of the cuff – along the lower edge of the interfacing – to the wrong side. Catch-stitch the hem as above. Turn the sleeve right-side out and turn up the cuff.

Separate cuffs
1 Interface half the width of the cuff.

2 Fold with right sides together, and stitch the short seam at each end. Trim, turn and press (*Figure 135*).

3 Stitch the single thickness of the cuff to the sleeve, matching the ends together at the back-arm line of the sleeve – about 5 cm from the sleeve seam (*Figure 136*). Layer the seam turnings and press them upwards inside the sleeve.

4 Turn up the cuff. Turn the facing inside the sleeve and catch-stitch as above.

Sleeve bands
These need to be set below a sleeve opening.

1 Interface and make the bands as for separate cuffs, first working any bound buttonhole as on page 54.

2 Stitch the interfaced edge to the sleeve, letting the overlap extend beyond the opening.

3 Turn in the seam allowance of the band facing, and slip-hem to the previous seamline (*Figure 137*). Complete the buttonhole as on page 62.

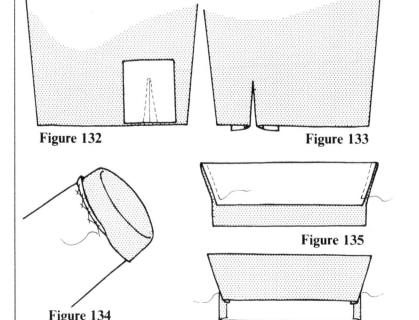

Figure 132   **Figure 133**    **Figure 136**

Figure 135

Figure 134   **Figure 137**

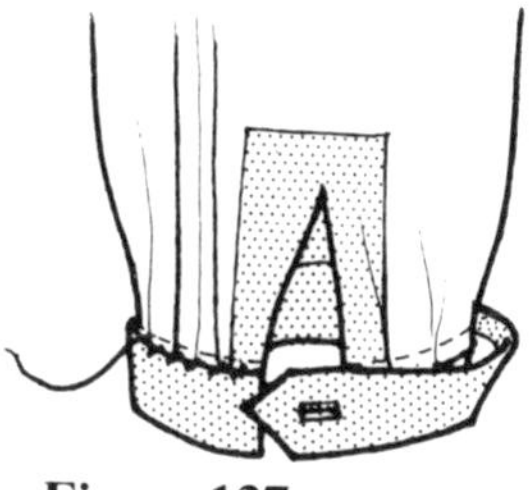

MAKING UP THE JACKET

SETTING IN THE SLEEVES

Even in thick fabric, setting in a sleeve is simpler than it looks, and far easier than the complicated collar and pockets which you have already tackled.

1 Turn the jacket inside out. Put the sleeve (right-side out) inside the jacket, matching the underarm seams. Check by the notches that you have the sleeve in its proper armhole – the double notch identifies the back edge (*Figure 138*).

2 Pin together from the underarm seam up to the notches.

3 Pin the centre of the sleevehead to the shoulder seam. Spread the fullness to fit, and pin.

4 Tack, and remove the pins.

5 Try on the jacket. The sleeve should hang without wrinkles. If there should be creases pulling from the front of the armhole, and loose folds at the back, as in *Figure 139*, then move the fullness slightly towards the front of the armhole. If the creases pull from behind the shoulder and there are loose folds in front (*Figure 140*) then move the fullness slightly towards the back of the armhole. Tack the altered position.

6 Stitch the armhole seam, beginning at the underarm seam, and finishing by overlapping a few stitches.

7 Press the turnings *lightly*, towards the sleeve.

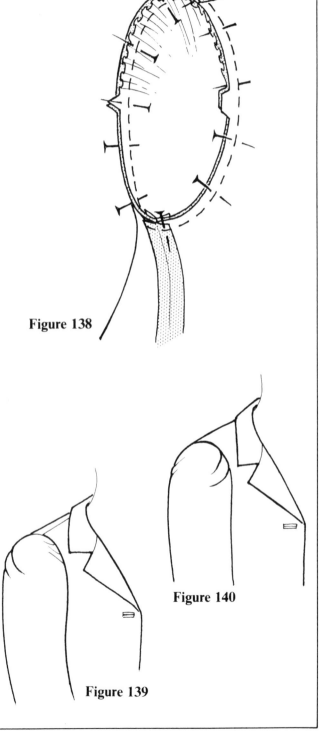

Figure 138

Figure 140

Figure 139

MAKING UP THE JACKET

HEM FINISH

For a plain hem

1 Cut strips of interfacing 3 cm wide and press to the wrong side of the jacket hemline, just above the hem allowance.

2 Turn up and tack the hem. Press lightly.

3 Fold the lower ends of the facings over the hem, trimming away surplus fabric inside the facing (*Figure 141*).

4 Slip-hem the bottom of the facing to the jacket, and herringbone-stitch the raw edge of the facing up to the top of the hem. Catch-stitch the hem as in *Figure 134*.

For a drawstring waist

1 Make a hand-worked buttonhole 5 cm from each front edge, just above the hem allowance. (For these buttonholes, see pages 62 and 63.)

2 Turn up the 5 cm hem allowance. Fold the facing back over the hem.

3 Machine the hem (*Figure 142*).

4 Thread the waistline with cord, or with a rouleau of the fabric. Rouleaux are cut on the bias, seamed and turned right side out as in *Figure 143*. The strips should be cut 5 to 7 cm wide, according to the thickness of the material. It is easier to turn a jersey than a woven fabric. Either pull through with a safety pin or else stitch across one end and push with the knob of a knitting needle.

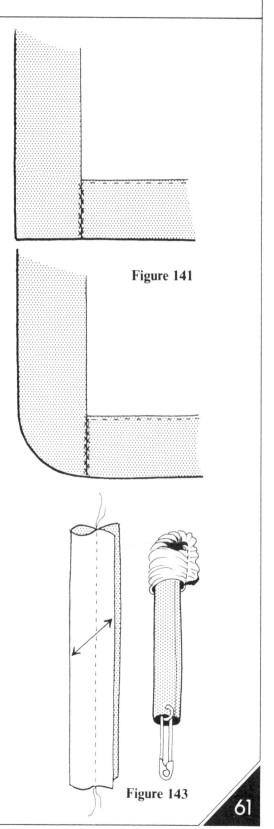

Figure 141

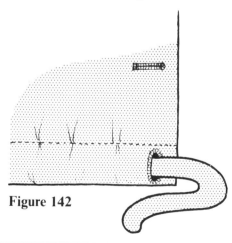

Figure 142

Figure 143

BOUND BUTTONHOLES: SECOND STAGE

1 Pin the facing accurately behind the buttonhole as worked in *Figures 112–116*.

2 Through the buttonhole, cut a corresponding slit in the facing.

3 Turn in the edges of the facing narrowly, and hem to the binding (*Figure 144*).

HAND-WORKED BUTTONHOLES

1 Tack the jacket and facing together round each buttonhole position.

2 Punch a hole with a stiletto or knitting needle at the outer end of the buttonhole.

3 Machine 0·2 cm above and below the buttonhole marking (*Figure 145*). Cut the buttonhole open.

4 With buttonhole twist, work from right to left from the inner end of the buttonhole. *Figure 146* shows how the needle is inserted from behind the buttonhole edge, and how the thread from the needle eye is twisted from the right, under the needle and back over it. Pull the knot upwards to the edge. Work the stitches very closely together.

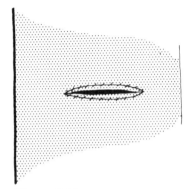

Figure 144

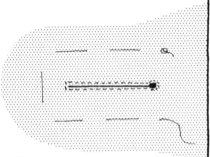

Figure 145

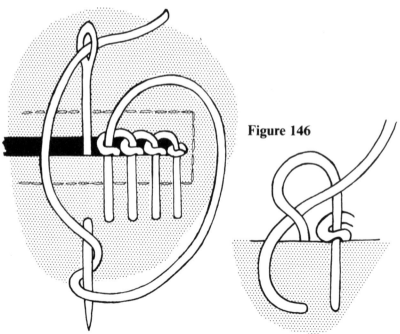

Figure 146

4 At the outer end of the buttonhole, work the stitches fan-wise round the punched hole, then work back along the other side.

5 Make two satin-stitches across the inner end of the buttonhole and work buttonhole stitches over them (*Figure 147*).

BUTTONS

With button thread or buttonhole twist, sew buttons to correspond to the buttonholes, down the left front. Make the thread shank long enough to raise the button well above the fabric, so that the jacket will fasten without dimpling at each buttonhole (*Figure 148*).

ARROWHEADS

These can be worked to finish the ends of bound pockets, as in the photograph on page 42, or at the top of a jacket back pleat. Mark the triangular outline with chalk. Work with buttonhole twist, keeping the stitches closely together (*Figure 149*).

Bring the needle up at the bottom left-hand corner and take a tiny stitch across the top. Take the next stitch across the base and continue with longer stitches across the top and shorter ones across the base, until the triangle is filled.

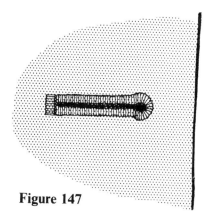

Figure 147

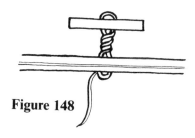

Figure 148

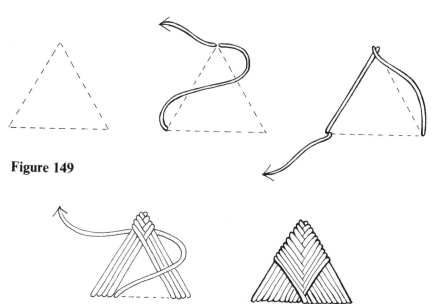

Figure 149

THE LINING

1 First sew in any shoulder-pads, to the jacket seam allowances.

2 Stitch the lining darts, and yoke, shoulder and side seams. Press a 1 cm pleat down the centre-back. Stitch across the pleat at waist level.

3 Stitch the lining sleeve seams, but do not set in the sleeves yet.

4 To sew the lining in by hand, fold under the seam allowances, clip as necessary, tack and fell to the facings from centre-back round and down to hemline. (It helps to put the jacket on inside out and get a friend to pin the lining in place.)

5 To set in by machine, place jacket and lining right sides together, match the edges of facings and lining and stitch. Turn right-side out through the hemline.

6 Tack the lining to the jacket seam allowances round the armholes.

7 Turn up and fell the hem, being sure to leave at least 1 cm ease in the length of the lining so that it does not pull. At the bottom of the facings, this ease will form a small pleat (*Figure 150*).

8 Turn the jacket sleeves inside out. Slip the lining sleeves over them, right-side out. Turn in and fell the wrist edge 3 cm above the hem edge of the jacket.

9 At the sleevehead, turn in the lining seam allowance and fell to the armhole turnings of jacket and lining. Allow at least 1 cm ease in the length of the sleeve lining (*Figure 151*).

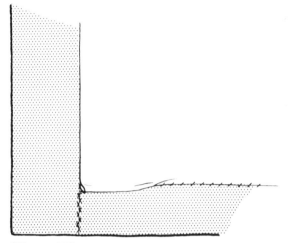

Figure 150

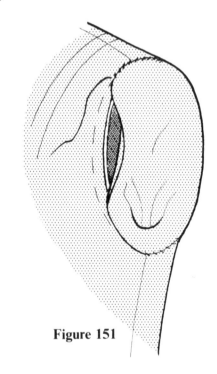

Figure 151